Keeping
Her Keys

An Introduction to Hekate's
Modern Witchcraft

Keeping Her Keys

An Introduction to Hekate's Modern Witchcraft

Cyndi Brannen

MOON BOOKS

Winchester, UK
Washington, USA

JOHN HUNT PUBLISHING

First published by Moon Books, 2019
Moon Books is an imprint of John Hunt Publishing Ltd., No. 3 East Street, Alresford
Hampshire SO24 9EE, UK
office@jhpbooks.com
www.johnhuntpublishing.com
www.moon-books.net

For distributor details and how to order please visit the 'Ordering' section on our website.

ISBN: 978 1 78904 075 3
978 1 78904 076 0 (ebook)
Library of Congress Control Number: 2018940335

A CIP catalogue record for this book is available from the British Library.

Design: Stuart Davies

UK: Printed and bound by CPI Group (UK) Ltd, Croydon, CR0 4YY
US: Printed and bound by Thomson-Shore, 7300 West Joy Road, Dexter, MI 48130

We operate a distinctive and ethical publishing philosophy in
all areas of our business, from our global network of authors to
production and worldwide distribution.

Contents

A Witch's Prayer to Hekate

Mighty Hekate, Queen of the Witches,
Blessed am I,
To call myself one of your chosen.
Mighty Hekate, Queen of the Witches,
You are both the dark and the light.
You are the way,
And You are the light along it.
My Queen, Holder of the keys of all creation.
Mighty Hekate, Queen of the Witches,
I stand before you in this liminal space,
That you created for us alone.
Here in this place of the in-between,
I feel the energy of the worlds,
I see the vision of the future,
I hold the wisdom of the past.

Mighty Hekate, Queen of the Witches,
You have bestowed upon me the power of the Witch.
Through the gifts of Your sacred keys,
I am the walker between the worlds,
The spinner of the web of fate,
The knower of Your secrets,
The student of Your mysteries,
The giver of Your healing.

Mighty Hekate, Queen of the Witches,
My journey is a blessed one,
Each key you give me unlocks great power,
Grateful I am for all Your keys;
The key of acceptance for that which I cannot change,
The key of courage to overcome adversity,
The key of kindness for myself and others,

They key of pain through which I discover my own strength,
The key of suffering in which I found healing,
The key of peace that brings me contentment,
The key of wisdom so that I may live a life of truth.

Mighty Hekate, Queen of the Witches,
My witch's journey is a blessing,
Through the darkness of the Under World,
Up to the heights of the heavens,
And the balance of everyday life.
Through all situations, I honor You.
In all ways, I honor You.
For all of time, Eternal Queen, I honor You.

Exercises

Setting up Your Witch Journal
Commitment Ritual
Applying the Principles
A Magical Life is an Intentional One
Unifying the Three Selves Meditation
Centering
Processing an Encounter with Hekate
World Soul Journey
Establishing a Daily Meditation Practice
Feeling the Power of the Epithets
Starting Your Book of Shadows
Evoking Hekate
Dark Moon Ritual
Writing a Noumenia Intentional Prayer
Making Hekate's Wheel of the Year
Making a Strophalos
Using Hekate's Symbols
Adding Color to the Wheel of the Year
Experiencing the Energy of Hekate's Colors
Correspondence Quest
Making the Three Keys Incense
Hekate and the Major Arcana
Establishing a Daily Tarot Practice
Intentional Lucid Dreaming
Completing Your Altar
Casting Hekate's Wheel
Writing and Casting Your Own Spell

Activities

Blessings, Chants, Hymns and Prayers

A Witch's Prayer to Hekate
Prayer for a New Beginning
Prayer to Hekate for a Magical Life
Anima Mundi Chant
Three Keys Chant
The Orphic Hymn to Hekate
Blessing of Hekate's Wheel of the Year
Strophalos Blessing
Prayer to Hekate, Soul of the World
Prayer to Hekate, Mistress of Balance on the Spring Equinox
Hymn to Hekate the Powerful on the Summer Solstice
Prayer to Hekate of the Harvest on the Fall Equinox
Hekate Kourotrophos: Blessing of Children
Prayer to Hekate the Storm Bringer
Prayer to Hekate, Goddess of the Under World

Introduction

In October 2017, I started writing about what I call Modern Hekatean Witchcraft that's a combination of Hekate and Applied Modern Witchcraft. Modern Hekatean Witchcraft is all about Hekate, practicing witchcraft, and personal development work. In my blog, Keeping Her Keys, I offered "how-to-if-you-want-to" articles about creating sacred space, using Hekate's many epithets, devotional practices, and Hekatean focused witchery. The blog grew quickly as did the Facebook page associated with it. I had just wanted to write about my own perspective as a devotee of Hekate, witch, mom, survivor, etc., but what I was saying resonated with lots of people. I see myself as a voice of the Modern Hekatean Witchcraft movement. We're all in this together. People kept asking me where my book was, so I thought it best to write one. *Keeping Her Keys: An Introduction to Modern Hekatean Witchcraft* is that book.

Keeping Her Keys Your Way

The structure of this course is flexible. One of the central tenets of my take on Modern Hekatean Witchcraft is a "you do you" approach. I wrote this book to provide guidance and information for all of you Keepers. I wrote the book I wanted to read.

Modern Hekatean Witchcraft

This book is an introductory course about Modern Hekatean Witchcraft. This isn't a tradition and you won't be asked to join a coven or other form of religious organization. You'll learn by reading the content, exploring different concepts and practice techniques and methods for developing in all these areas. At the end of the course, you can become a Keeper of Her Keys through self-initiation. You can become a Priest or Priestess of your own temple if that works for you. Once you complete self-initiation you'll be referred to as a Guide in the Keeping Her Keys community and you will be able to mentor students taking this course. Lesson Two describes the Keeping Her Keys framework in detail.

My Witch's Journey

Many practitioners of Modern Hekatean Witchcraft report they felt called by Hekate in a very profound way. I'm no different. My experience happened while doing the laundry (of all things!). As I was folding towels, I clearly heard a calm self-assured woman's voice say, "it's time." In an instant, I was immersed in a feeling of pure love and complete acceptance. My limited knowledge of Hekate was that She was a dark goddess of witches. I resisted Her call for months. Eventually, my life reached a point when I turned to Her. I fell on my knees and begged, "Help me." She did. The Dark Mother guided me out of my personal Under World.

During this time the practice of what would become the Keeping Her Keys framework was developing, I was teaching personal development from a witchy perspective. This included local events and online ones. I called this venture Open Circle and the program I developed is known as The Sacred Seven. However, my personal life was a hot mess. Divorce, financial ruin, personal illness, and other disasters were commonplace during those years. I did the personal development work necessary to reclaim my life through my own efforts and Hekate's guidance. There were times I thought I'd never get through everything, but, here I am having written this book.

Overview of this Book

And here you are, reading this book. That's the last time I'm going to call it that because this is really an introductory course to Modern Hekatean Witchcraft. You probably have your own story about how you found Hekate. Perhaps, like me, She found you when you needed Her the most. This is a common theme from the countless stories I've heard about when Hekate calls a devotee for the first time. She stands at the gate, extending a new key. It is up to us to take that key and use it. Personal agency, our ability to change our lives for the better, is a central belief of Modern Hekatean Witchcraft.

I write more about my approach to witchcraft (which I call the Keeping Her Keys framework) in the second lesson after a summary of the common themes of Modern Hekatean Witchcraft discussed in the first. In the third lesson I write about communicating with Hekate, including what to do when Hekate calls us for the first time. Not everyone has this experience, so I also make recommendations for seeking Her either for the first time or the hundredth. In the fourth lesson, we review the fascinating history of Hekate as well as our contemporary understanding.

A main feature of Modern Hekatean Witchcraft is the use of epithets in devotion and witchery. Hekate has over two hundred characteristics based on ancient texts and modern interpretations. In the fifth Lesson, I discuss these epithets and how to use them. In the following lesson you'll learn about honoring Hekate, while in the seventh lesson we discuss Hekate's Wheel of the Year. In Lesson Eight, Hekate's symbols are presented. Lesson Nine introduces you to the correspondences of Modern Hekatean Witchcraft and how to use them. Then we move onto a discussion about Hekate's garden.

In Lesson 11, you'll learn the basics of divination within Modern Hekatean Witchcraft with an emphasis on establishing a daily Tarot practice. Then onto Lesson 12 where we discuss natural and created types of sacred space, including how to create various kinds. The final lesson of the course provides you will all you need to know about crafting spells Modern Hekatean Witchcraft style.

The last part of this course is a discussion about self-initiation.

While this course is not part of a tradition, your completion of it represents a substantial training in Modern Hekatean Witchcraft. As such, you'll have the opportunity to complete the initiation process to become a Guide in the Keeping Her Keys community. You can personally acknowledge yourself as a Keeper of Her Keys.

About this Course

Within each lesson, you'll find many activities and exercises. Everything in the course has been tried by members of the Keeping Her Keys community. I've used their feedback to refine them. You can use them as presented, adapt them to suit yourself, or as a source of inspiration to make up your own based on the principles you've learned. The Keeping Her Keys online community offers support and further resources for this course.

Course Timeline

This course should commence on the first day of the lunar cycle, the astrological New Moon. The reason for this will become clear as you work through the content. I recommend using the lunar cycle as a guide for when you start each lesson, starting on the first day and ending on the last day. I've designed the book to take an entire calendar year plus one day to complete, in the tradition of witch training. In the suggested schedule, I am using "cycle" to refer to the 28-day lunar cycle. There are approximately 13 lunar cycles in one calendar year.

Recommended Schedule
Cycle 1: Introduction, Lesson 1 and 2
Cycle 2: Lesson 3
Cycle 3: Lesson 4
Cycle 4: Lesson 5
Cycle 5: Lesson 6
Cycle 6: Lesson 7

Exercises

The exercises for this course are designed to help you learn more about Modern Hekatean Witchcraft and prepare you for initiation as a Keeper of Her Keys. The journaling prompts are there to guide you with processing what you're learning, but you should write down thoughts as they occur to you during this course and make notes as you go along. Write as much or as little as you need to complete any exercise, journal prompt, etc. Feel free to use point form, charts, tables, bulleted lists, or long paragraphs – whatever works for you.

Let's Begin

I am honored to be writing about Hekate, witchcraft, and personal development. *Keeping Her Keys: An Introduction to Modern Hekatean Witchcraft* was truly a labor of love. Perhaps even Hekate Herself helped guide my fingers on the keyboard! I hope you enjoy reading this book as much as I did writing it.

Exercise: Setting Up Your Witch Journal

Timing: Prior to the Dark Moon, with enough time to prepare your journal.

Intent: Create a personal record of your experiences during this course.

Objective: Understand the importance of keeping a record of your experiences.

Start by picking a notebook that's easy to use and durable. I recommend a hard-back spiral bound one, but there are so many options to choose from. Whatever you select, make sure it's easy to carry with you since you'll be keeping it with you during spells and rituals. You might also want to take it everywhere, so you can record your thoughts about the content and the exercises when they come to you. I'm a big believer in keeping journals. I have multiple ones on the go – one for recording things related to Keeping Her Keys, another is my personal journal, and still another one for business type things. I don't like to mix business with witchcraft, at least not in the same notebook! You should have a dedicated journal just for this book or at least for Modern Hekatean Witchcraft. How you organize your Keeping Her Keys journal is up to you. I use those easy stick tabs that can be written on to make it easy to find the different lessons. You can use these tabs to mark passages of the book you want to keep track of, too. I use different colored pens for different types of writing. For example, I use red ink to record quotes from the ancient texts but black ink for my own words. You can also make a title page for your journal using images, symbols, epithets and correspondences of Hekate. Before moving onto the next lesson, make sure your journal is ready to go because you'll start writing in it.

Summary

This book will provide you with an introduction to the type of Modern Hekatean Witchcraft that I practice and call Keeping Her Keys. This new framework focuses on devotion to Hekate, witchcraft, and personal development. The idea grew out of my blog, *Keeping Her Keys*. I started the blog because I couldn't find the resources needed to help with my version of what I started calling Modern Hekatean Witchcraft. Soon after the blog started, people began contacting me looking for my book. So, I got busy writing one. In my blog, I write a lot about my own *witch's journey.* This book is the next step on my path and a beginning for you. Let's begin!

Hail Hekate! Brightest Blessings,

Cyndi

Lesson 1: Modern Hekatean Witchcraft

Modern Hekatean Witchcraft is firmly rooted in the present although many of the practitioners are students of the ancient writings. This is Applied Modern Witchcraft with Hekate. The difference is that we aren't attempting to reconstruct the past, but we adapt historical documents and practices for use in the twenty-first century. We often start from scratch, making things up as we go and working on divine inspiration. The modern interpretation of Hekate as Maiden, Mother and Crone is an excellent example. Another aspect of Modern Hekatean Witchcraft that is completely modern is the emphasis on personal development. For me, being a psychologist, personal development is a huge part of my private devotion and witchery as well as my public teaching and writing. I would argue that modern psychology is at the heart of Modern Hekatean Witchcraft – many practitioners focus on things such as living an authentic life, being a better person, healing from trauma, improving relationships, career advancement and other similar very modern concepts. One other modern concept that distinguishes Modern Hekatean Witchcraft from other forms of devotion to Hekate is that it has such a strong progressive social agenda that I seriously considered calling it Progressive Hekatean Witchcraft. Many practitioners of Modern Hekatean Witchcraft are committed to making the world better for themselves, their loved ones, and the vulnerable. The evidence is found in the countless posts, blogs, articles and other sources advocating for social justice in Her name. Examples range from making donations to charities as an act of devotion to public activism.

At the core of Modern Hekatean Witchcraft is working with Hekate. How you interpret Hekate is entirely up to you. Within Modern Hekatean Witchcraft, She is understood as everything from an energetic force to a female humanoid goddess. Becoming a Hekatean, a practitioner who works with Hekate, is serious business. This course will provide you will what you need to start your journey. As experienced followers will attest, She is a rather demanding deity. Hekate chooses Her children because She knows that they can serve Her well. Like the adage, to whom She gives much, much is expected. Within Modern Hekatean Witchcraft this expectation consists of scholarship, sharing knowledge, devotional practice, community service and living a magical life. Working with Hekate has many diverse forms, just as She does. Her many epithets and roles provide a rich source of information for practicing devotion and witchcraft. Her role as Queen of the Under World is particularly important within Modern Hekatean Witchcraft because it demonstrates Her commitment to the darkness within each of us. Beyond Her Under World aspects, many practitioners of Modern Hekatean Witchcraft connect with other epithets such as *Triformis* (good for personal transformation), *Enodia* (for your personal journey), and *Kourotrophos* (Guardian of Children). Practitioners of Modern Hekatean Witchcraft recognize Hekate as *The World Soul* and *Pammetor* (Mother of All). We believe that she is omnipresent, omnipotent, and all powerful. That is not to say that we feel subservient to Hekate, but rather we find freedom in Her mighty powers. Finally, it's important to say that Modern Hekatean Witchcraft practitioners have a personal relationship with Hekate as they understand Her. Although the nature of the relationship varies greatly, the common theme includes performing rituals that honor Hekate on a regular basis.

Speaking of the benefits, the final key of Modern Hekatean Witchcraft is the active practice of witchcraft. This can take many forms, but the common element is that we seek Hekate's energy to help us manipulate the natural forces of the world to achieve a desired goal. Witchcraft is a combination of skill, knowledge, belief and power. All these work together to produce a mighty spell. Anyone can become a witch although some are born with more natural ability than others. One of the hefty perks of practicing Modern Hekatean Witchcraft is the development of highly effective witchery through the emphasis on highly effective personal development practices and witchery. Specific activities can include spells, rituals, meditative journeying and prayers. The common focus is petitioning Hekate to lend her favor to our desires. Another theme I've noticed is that many practitioners use practical magic that relies on initiative, effort and using what's on hand rather than relying on prescribed spells and ornate tools. Within Modern Hekatean Witchcraft, I've noticed a collective focus on using witchcraft to help us solve our own problems. Hekate cannot do for us what She can't do through us. Modern Hekatean Witchcraft reflects this motto. We seek to be better people, make wise decisions, and ask for her guidance rather than sit on our hands and expect Her to do the work for us.

Flexibility and Change

In addition to the Three Keys, another central theme of Modern Hekatean Witchcraft is that just as we change, so does our understanding of Hekate and so does our witchcraft. There's an energy of learning common in practitioners across the globe. The more we learn, the more we grow. Hekate reflects those who work with Her – She, too, has changed since the beginning of time, at least in how we perceive Her. As practitioners, we must be flexible in our beliefs and ways – rigidity doesn't serve Our Lady or ourselves well at all. It also blocks us from sincere devotion and vastly limits our witchcraft.

Come One, Come All

Another thing I've noticed is that Modern Hekatean Witchcraft is very inclusive. If you feel called or are seeking Hekate, then you are welcome to hop on the bus. You can be a mostly monotheist like me or worship as many deities as you see fit, you can be focused on one aspect of Her or a scholar of Her many epithets, you can be in the broom closet or a pentacle-wearing priestess. Come one, come all.

We're All Just Bozos on the Hekate Bus

I'm concluding this introductory lesson by talking a bit about one of the personality characteristics I've noticed in practitioners – humility. Yes. We're not a group of high brows looking down on the mere mortals. There's an acknowledgement among us doing Modern Hekatean Witchcraft that we are *all just bozos on the Hekate bus*. None of us is better than anyone else. We're trying our best. We're not perfect. We know we're misfits, rebels and weirdos. We like it that way, but we're not going to brag about it.

The Holy Darkness is Nigh

As you'll read in the lesson on the Wheel of the Year, November is given special attention. This is due to the multiple celebrations in Her honor during this month and because of the long nights here in the Northern Hemisphere. We can interpret this as the age of the Holy Darkness, the time when the Divine Feminine (including Hekate) reclaim their position in the lives of their chosen, but also in a shift in society. Using Holy Darkness to describe this time is fitting because of the imagery of Hekate as the Torch-Bearer shining Her light along our way, with the moon also shining upon us. The moon is the symbol of feminine energy, too. The Holy Darkness extends to the entire age that we are living in. I feel the tremendous interest in devotion to Hekate right now reflects Her rise to energetic prominence that we are currently experiencing. Her Holy Darkness is spreading all over the world – across cultures, languages, genders, etc. I can't explain it, but I can feel it. Modern Hekatean Witchcraft has emerged just when it's most needed. It's almost as though

Hekate guided us to create it to meet the growing need for teaching of new initiates and for healing ourselves and the world. I'm offering up this book as a way of helping to fill the void of information about practicing Modern Hekatean Witchcraft.

Understanding: Holy Darkness

I've just written about what I call the "Holy Darkness" referring to Hekate's rise in popularity amongst witches, pagans and others. In general, this can be interpreted as part of the return of the Divine Feminine to mainstream culture. How has the Holy Darkness manifested in your life? What does the Holy Darkness mean to you? What signs of it do you see in your own life? How about in society? Why is the term "Holy Darkness" a good way to characterize this shift in your own life, other practitioners and even in society?

The Benefits of Modern Hekatean Witchcraft

I hope this introduction has shown you some advantages of taking this introductory course on Modern Hekatean Witchcraft. Another benefit that I haven't mentioned before is the tremendous one of being a witch, or if you're not comfortable with that title, then of learning about witchcraft. Equal parts mystery, science and experience, witchcraft as a practice will strengthen you in ways that you haven't yet imagined. By learning to work with natural energies and Hekate, we develop skills for self-discipline and manifestation that will help us lead more fulfilling lives. Witchcraft is a source of healing for many. Sometimes it's through the application of magic, but often is through learning that we recover from our past wounds. Witchcraft is ultimately about claiming our personal power and standing firmly in it.

Exercise: Commitment Ritual

In this ritual, you'll be making a personal commitment to completing this course, for using your learning for your own development and for the best interests of others. Any ritual is an extension of an intention. Indeed, all of witchcraft is based on the notion that the intention is the most important part of any working. Perhaps you are already familiar with this idea. Setting intentions is a vital part of witchcraft, so it's fitting that you begin your journey by setting your intentions to this course now.

Guidelines for Writing Intentions

I talk a lot about the importance of well developed intentions throughout this course. A strong intention needs to be very specific and use as few words as possible. An intention is a way of summarizing our desired outcome. By going through the process of thinking about what we hope to achieve, we can narrow our focus to exactly what we want. The more precise an intention, the more effective the spell. Broad spells that ask for generic things often fail because there is too much ambiguity. Whether we are manipulating natural energy or petitioning Hekate for Her assistance, the clearer we are with our intention, the more apt we are to use energy to our advantage or to receive Hekate's help. The best example of how an imprecise spell can lead to undesirable results comes from a student of mine. She desperately wanted a position as a veterinary assistant, so she did a spell to manifest a job working with cats. She got a job alright – working at a discount store with a giant tiger for its logo! Her desire did not match her magical intention. Don't let this happen to you.

In addition to their magical proficiency, specific intentions help to activate our behaviors, thoughts, and emotions towards manifesting our desired outcome. We'll be motivated to do all we can to manifest our goal. Thus, a great intention brings into alignment our magic, actions, feelings, and thoughts. With this powerful combination, how can our spells fail?

Steps for Developing a Great Intention

- Write down all your initial ideas.
- Once you've got them all down, study them for common themes. Connect the themes using lines or circles. Whatever makes sense to you.
- Next, use these common themes to identify the main intention. Be as precise as possible.
- Write the one intention on a separate piece of paper. Be very specific and use as few words as possible. You may want to write your intention on a piece of durable paper since you'll be posting it somewhere to remind you of the intention while you work your way through this book. If you're so inclined, you can use decorative paper (there are lots out there that have keys on them) or decorate a plain sheet using symbols of Hekate. I usually do the latter. While I'm making the symbols, I concentrate on my intention and develop the words for the rituals and make an action plan.
- Here are some suggestions that may be helpful in determining your intention for this course:
  o What do I hope to learn from this course?
  o How will I be transformed by this course?
  o How will I use what I learn from this course?

Course Commitment Ritual

Once you've determined your intentions, it's time to do a short commitment ritual. For this ritual, you'll need a candle of some sort, preferably white. It's fine if its battery operated – not everyone can have an open flame in their homes. You'll also need a single sheet of paper to write your intention on. It's helpful to have an image or symbol of Hekate, too. This can be something you've drawn or printed from the computer.

Requirements

o   Your intention written on a single sheet of paper
o   White candle
o   Image or symbol of Hekate

Directions

• Find a quiet place where you can be alone for 15–30 minutes. We'll have an in-depth discussion about sacred space in Lesson 10. For now, ensure that you have a clean and quiet area.
• Wash up before beginning.
• Set your candle, intention, and representation of Hekate near each other in a clean space.
• Light the candle. Say, "I light this candle to activate my intention for this course." Read your specific intention.
• While holding your intention in both hands, hold it towards the sky and say, "may my intellect work to realize this intention." Now point your hands towards the ground and say, "may my emotions work to realize this intention." Finally, hold your hands over your heart center and say, "may my actions work to realize this intention."
• Now turn to the symbol of Hekate while holding the paper near the flame, saying, "I release this intention into Your Hands, Mighty Hekate, may you guide my thoughts, feelings, and actions so that I manifest my desired outcome."
• Pause for a few moments so you can contemplate your intention being released into Hekate's hands. She may speak to you regarding your intention for this book. If She does come forward, make sure you write about the experience in your journal.
• Once you complete releasing your intention, thank Hekate and extinguish the flame.
• Write about your experience during this ritual in your journal.

- Keep the intention in a spot where you'll see it several times a day – on your bedroom mirror or bulletin board near your workspace.
- You can adapt this ritual for any type of manifestation work.

Prayer

Praying is a central part of my personal practice. What is a prayer? It's simply a spoken – even in your own head – request to any type of metaphysical entity. I pray for guidance, to express gratitude or to petition for Our Lady's intervention. When I pray, I create a connection between ourselves and the divine, in our case Hekate using what's known as active praying. My prayers are active because they not only establish a connection with Hekate but also contain affirmations for our commitment to bringing forth the subject of the prayer. This is different from passive praying when a person asks a god for whatever it is they desire and then does nothing on their own to manifest their intention. This type of prayer is about establishing what I need from Hekate to get the job done and what I'm going to do. As such, my prayers include a list of attributes (e.g., "May I be strong") or activities (e.g., "May I take Your key). I ask for Hekate's assistance with achieving the subject of the prayer. For example, I say "Shine Your light upon my path," as a way of asking for Her guidance. Basically, words without actions are meaningless. So, prayers are a commitment to action and to ask for Hekate's help. If we're not willing to do the work to achieve our desired outcome, then why should we think that She would? If the word "prayer" leaves a funny taste in your mouth, I totally understand. Call them incantations if that's more comfortable.

The importance of action runs through all the various parts of Modern Hekatean Witchcraft. It's vital for you to develop your own prayers, rituals, journeys, and spells. And why it's integral for you to interpret Hekate, witchcraft, and personal development work in ways that make the most sense to you. My prayer for this course is that it will help you along your personal journey.

Prayer for a New Beginning

There are several energetic activities that help get a project off to a great start. The first two you already did – develop a clear intention and then perform a ritual to activate the intention. Saying a blessing over the new venture, such as the *Prayer for a New Beginning* also helps. You can revise it however you wish, but I urge you to say some sort of prayer even if it's not this exact one. Feel free to use this prayer as a blessing over any beginning you undertake. The key being referred to in the prayer is for your journey with this course. Before you start reciting the prayer, take a few moments to calm yourself by taking deep, relaxing breaths.

Hail Hekate, She who holds the Keys.
Hail Hekate, She who lights the World.
Hail Hekate, She who stands at the Gate.
I stand before you, humbled by your blessing of a new key,
That opens the gate to a new beginning.
Accept my gratitude for bringing me to this place.
May I be brave enough to take up the key.
May I be committed enough to do the required work.
May I be strong enough to overcome all obstacles.
I ask for Your continued blessing,
Your guidance,
And protection,
So that I will be true to my path ahead.
Hail Hekate, She who holds the Keys.
Hail Hekate, She who lights the World.
Hail Hekate, She who stands at the Gate.

Practice: Witch's Hour of Power

Setting intentions and engaging in active prayer help to align ourselves with the outcomes we will manifest. There are many other strategies built into this course that will help you do the same. These strategies will enhance your personal development, help you lead a magical life and become much more effective with your witchcraft. You'll also develop a deeper understanding of Hekate and Her energy currents. Because Hekate is both an external force and the divine within each of us, all devotional work also is personal development. Through meditation, intention setting, self-checks, devotional work, journaling and other aspects of magical living you'll change throughout the course. The goal is to make you more you, not change who you are. The activities are designed to take about an hour a day. I call them the Witch's Hour of Power because doing them connects you to your power and enhances it. However, we all live busy lives, so the strategies are designed to take about one hour per day. The techniques are introduced throughout the course, but here's a summary of what we'll be covering:

- Affirmations
- Gratitude
- Journaling
- Intention Setting
- Meditation
- Self-Checks
- Tarot Practice

Summary

Modern Hekatean Witchcraft is an emerging movement that emphasizes individual interpretations of both devotion to Hekate and practicing witchcraft. Although this movement is very personalized, there are some common features: it is not a reconstructionist perspective, and it is very inclusive. There are three main keys of Modern Hekatean Witchcraft: working with Hekate, practicing witchcraft, and interpreting both through the lens of contemporary life. In addition, there is a great deal of flexibility in how practitioners interpret and apply the ancient texts and modern writing about Hekate, as well as a consensus that our understanding of Hekate can change over time. There's also a spirit of camaraderie amongst practitioners, a true sense of being all in this together. This movement has risen in conjunction with the return of Hekate to energetic dominance in our world, referred to as the Holy Darkness. Practicing Hekate's Modern Witchcraft has many benefits, including becoming better magical practitioners. Ritual is a central part of practicing Modern Hekatean Witchcraft, so we begin this course with a Commitment Ritual. Another key part of Hekate's Modern Witchcraft is prayers. Appropriately, the end of this first lesson includes a Prayer for a New Beginning.

Lesson 2: Keeping Her Keys

Keeping Her Keys is a framework for practicing Modern Hekatean Witchcraft. I wrote that it's a "framework" rather than a "tradition" because the latter implies a rigid structure while, to me, the former implies a flexible design. Keeping Her Keys is just that – flexible. Use the content of this book as you feel led. Change things up as you will. My mission is to make Modern Hekatean Witchcraft accessible to everyone who believes and is willing to do the work. This course is designed to be appropriate for anyone regardless of experience in witchcraft or paganism. I've made every effort to make this approach user-friendly for people of all orientations and paths. For example, unlike in some other Pagan traditions, there is no use of female and male energy or accompanying tools. Instead, we use the underlying energies that are typically associated with either masculinity or femininity, such as aggression or kindness. It was my goal in developing this perspective that I do my best to make it as inclusive as possible. I hope I achieved that.

Working with Hekate

Hekate is at the very heart of the Keeping Her Keys approach to Modern Hekatean Witchcraft. Here are some of the characteristics that make it special:

- An emphasis on learning different epithets associated with Hekate and using them in devotion, witchcraft, and personal development work.
- A unique Wheel of the Year that is a guideline for various practices including devotion, witchcraft, and personal development work.
- Applying symbols and correspondences in new ways with Hekate that enhances magic.

Working with Hekate entails a close personal relationship, but it is not among equals. Hekate is viewed as all powerful, all knowing, and eternal. As such, Hekate will always be beyond us, but She is approachable, kind, and supportive. She is also fierce, demanding and a bit intimidating.

Perhaps the most important aspect of working with Hekate is that She is seen as a living Goddess that is completed through our devotion to Her. It is our commitment to Her that renders Her into a form that we can understand. While Her true nature is unknowable to us as humans, we can access Her divine energy currents through worship. Her energy currents are interpreted using Her many epithets, although we can approach Her as the World Soul containing all the possible types of energy available to us. When we think of Hekate as the source of all energy, we can focus on different aspects of the energy. We can express devotion to specific currents given the circumstances of our lives. In addition, it's possible for our understanding of Her energies to change over time. Finally, our personal understanding of Hekate will depend largely on which of Her energy currents – that we interpret as Her epithets – make the most sense to us. As a group, devotees complete Her with all our different ways of relating to Her. You will complete Her in the way that She reveals Herself to you.

We all filter Her personal presentation to us through the lens of our own understanding. Our filter includes our personality characteristics, experiences, and circumstances. For example, many devotees have been called by Hekate when we were at our darkest hour. As such, we have suffered through trauma, including abuse, violence, and invalidation. If Hekate initially presented Herself to us as our Savior out of these Under World experiences, then we are more likely to understand – or complete Her – as a Goddess of the Under World who guided us out of darkness than for someone who found Hekate out of curiosity. I hope this makes sense!

Given that our emphasis is on Hekate's energy currents, we can all interpret Her as we deem appropriate. Some of us may believe Her to have human form, while others see Her as a symbolic manifestation of the energy She represents. I don't see Her an ancient goddess who was defined thousands of years ago. I also believe that Hekate can't be put in a concrete box where we can pull Her out at our will. She is beyond our control; all we can do is seek Her attention and petition Her for blessings.

In ancient times, Hekate was not seen as being a crone goddess. There is no reference in antiquity to Her as an elderly wise woman. However, during the twentieth century, several different modern witchcraft perspectives began to see Her as a crone. Moreover, She was either the crone part of the Maiden, Mother, Crone framework for understanding the feminine divine or as all three parts of this triad. This was at least partially born out of ancient references that saw Hekate as one of a triad of moon goddesses and Her association with the number three. Thus, in our current collective understanding of Hekate, we see Her as Maiden, Mother, Crone or just Crone, but that this represents a new interpretation of Her. This common understanding arose from individual practitioners seeing Her this way. She became – or was completed as – the Maiden, Mother, Crone triad because people interpreted Her this way. A strictly reconstructionist approach would refuse to consider this a legitimate interpretation of Hekate. They would try to keep Her in their concrete box where She is defined only according to ancient scripts. Perhaps Hekate presents Herself to you in a way that hasn't yet become part of the public discourse. It's important to cultivate this understanding. Remember that the way you complete Her is entirely up to you.

Witchcraft

Just as our individual understanding of Hekate is filtered through our own personality, experiences, and circumstances, so is our practice of witchcraft. I see witchcraft as a living thing that is constantly evolving and adapting to our experiences and circumstances. This isn't to discredit traditional approaches to witchcraft, but to acknowledge that what worked in the past may not work in the present, or at least may need to be adapted for contemporary life. An example of this can be found in using witch jars for spells. Witch jars have long been part of a witch's repertoire for spell casting. A traditional witch jar would contain ingredients such as urine, plants, and maybe even animal parts. This isn't feasible for many of us in modern society, but we can access ingredients that share the same energetic properties and intentions as these historic ones.

I'm a firm believer that the rituals and spells we create – based on research and contemplation – are the most effective ones. Our witchery needs to be an extension of our personalities, experiences and our understanding of Hekate. In addition, our personal circumstances can influence the type of witchcraft that we do. Some of us can do workings out in nature, while others cast circles in their bedroom.

I put a lot of emphasis on using Hekate's many epithets – characteristics – witchcraft. For example, if you were to develop a spell to improve your work situation, you could call upon aspects of Hekate that would help you prepare for the position you want, an epithet that helps show you the sort of opportunity that you want, and one that would remove any barriers between you and your ideal job. We'll discuss how to use the epithets in witchery in detail later.

The Real Work

The commitment to actively pursuing personal development is what I call the Real Work. I've been teaching the Real Work as a pagan path for personal development for about a decade. Many of the techniques introduced in this book are based on that program. I call personal development the Real Work because only through actively pursuing becoming the most authentic version of ourselves can we truly be powerful in our lives and witchcraft.

Many of us are called by Hekate when we are broken. Through the exercises in this book, we can recover from our wounds and release the grip that the past can have on us. I also believe that each of us has a divine imprint that contains our full potential. Experiences such as trauma and invalidation can cause us to feel that we are not a divine creation; that there is something innately wrong with us. We need to reject this notion entirely for we are the children of Hekate, created in Her image and exactly as She means for us to be. The exercises in this book will help you get back to the place of true understanding of your life's purpose and who you really area so you can live a truly magical life of your own creation. After all, the only rule that matters in witchcraft is *know yourself*. It's through personal development work that we develop a true understanding of who we really are. When we are living as our authentic self, we stand in our power and become capable of fulfilling the divine destiny that Hekate placed upon us long before we were born into this life.

Living a Magical Life

Part of our personal development is to utilize our skills and talents so that we can live a magical life of our own creation. Although what this means varies, the common foundation lies in our practice of Modern Hekatean Witchcraft which gives us the tools necessary to live an authentic life, but also for our soul's progression. The guidelines for living a lifestyle favorable to Hekate dates all the way back to the ancient texts, particularly *The Chaldean Oracles.*[1] In this story, being virtuous is seen as vital for the soul's progression. Now what was defined as virtuous at the time the *Oracles* were channeled may not work in the modern world, but there are important lessons to learn from them.

Applying these ancient virtues to our contemporary values yields the three core principles that I believe to be central in the practice of Modern Hekatean Witchcraft.

Kindness

Being kind is so important in this world that we live in. By choosing to be kind to ourselves and others, we honor ourselves and Hekate. Moreover, we collectively create an energy current of kindness that is vital to overthrow the forces that seek to disempower the vulnerable in society. This is what is known as compassionate anger. Being kind is not a state of weakness, but of immense strength. We rely upon our integrity to fortify our kindness into a force of change in this world.

Integrity

Integrity is how I label our personal characteristics related to things like character and strength. Other aspects of integrity that are important include sincerity and dependability. Through our commitment to being sincere in all aspects of our lives we can learn to function as our authentic selves. If we're obliged to being sincere, then it becomes very difficult to go through life pretending to be something we're not. Being dependable means that we do what we say when we say we're going to do it. Like self-kindness, many of us are highly reliable when it comes to other people but aren't very good at keeping our word to ourselves. The commitment to being dependable must be applied to ourselves before anyone else.

Passion

The final core principle is passion for living a vibrant, authentic life. There is no room for accepting anything less than a magical life. The exercises in each of the lessons capitalize on the principle of passion by getting you busy doing things. This course is a busy, "take life by its horns" approach to devotion, witchcraft, and personal development. That's what Applied Modern Witchcraft is all about.

Adding Your Own Principles

Beyond these three core principles, add others that appeal to you. For example, you may feel drawn to have "strength" as a singular principle rather than having it under the umbrella of "integrity" because you are developing that aspect of your personality. You may have certain principles for a period and then move onto different ones. It's entirely up to you.

Exercise: Applying the Principles

For the first part of this journaling exercise, make a table with four columns. For the first column header write "Principle," for the second write "Examples," call the third one "Characteristics," and label the fourth "Development." Under the principle column, write down the first one – kindness. Next, underneath "Examples" describe a couple of times that you have been kind. It could be something like, "I was patient when my children threw a temper tantrum," or "I helped at the local animal shelter." Just provide enough details so that you can conjure up the feeling of kindness within yourself. Now looking at your examples, write down the specific characteristics you demonstrated in your examples of being kind. For example, if you kept your cool when your children were acting like monkeys, you displayed "patience," so you would put that down as a characteristic of kindness. The final column is where we identify aspects of a principle that we want to further develop. Maybe "patience" wasn't on your list of characteristics, so you might put that down in the "Development" column. Repeat this process for each of the other two principles. If you feel led, you can add additional principles that are part of your personal commitment to living a magical life.

The goals for this exercise are threefold:

- To get you thinking about just how you already display the three principles.

- To help you identify aspects of the principles that you can develop in your life. No one's perfect! By listing areas that you want to work on, it brings them forward in your life. You can save this exercise and revisit it from time to time to see how you're doing with your "Development" characteristics.

- The final objective of this exercise is to help you see that when we think about specific things, we also pull forward the energy associated with that thing. By thinking about passion, you probably actually started to feel a bit excited. Contemplating integrity often brings out our desire to live a sincere life. You may be feeling emotions, thoughts, and even contemplating certain actions after you complete the exercise. I wanted to introduce this concept using a simple exercise, so you can see for yourself the power of energy. We'll be using energy in many different forms and ways throughout this book.

Prayer to Hekate for a Magical Life

The prayer for this lesson focuses on seeking Hekate's support in your efforts to live a meaningful life. Feel free to recite the prayer as it is written or adapt it as you feel led. This short prayer can be added to your Witch's Hour of Power for your daily working with Hekate and as an affirmation.

Hail Hekate,
May I be ever passionate,
May I be kind to myself and others,
May I act with integrity.
Guardian, light my way.
Guide, show me how.
Gatekeeper, open the way
To a magical life.

Exercise: A Magical Life is an Intentional One

While living our principles certainly gives our lives meaning, it isn't by accident that we manifest the life we desire. The importance of intention is not limited to witchery, though. We can use the power of intention to help control outcomes in our regular activities and to set an energetic tone for our days. Intentions can be divided into two categories: internal and external. Internal intentions focus on our behaviors, feelings and thoughts. Learning to manage these is especially useful in challenging situations. For example, "I will be calm no matter what happens when I talk to _____." We can use intentions to govern our thoughts, as well. "Today, I will choose to think about happy times and not about _____" is a good technique for helping when dealing with the loss of a loved one. It may take an almost constant practice at first. However, this technique will work.

External intentions are those about manifesting a desired outcome that is not entirely in our hands. One of my go-to techniques is to set the intention of "this meeting will end with all items on the agenda resolved." I always set intentions for other events and for all my projects. Getting into the habit of intention setting is not only useful for everyday situations but helps us develop our ability to control energy. All emotions, thoughts and behaviors are energetic, as are outcomes in any situation. The more we practice selecting the type of energy we put out into the world and manifest, the stronger we become at using energy in our witchery.

Practice setting an intention for your day for one week. Start each morning with, "Today I am going to manifest _____" whatever your focus is for that day. Before an activity, especially meetings of all kinds, set your intention. Record your intentions and track your progress in your journal.

Being an Ethical Witch

While it's a great idea to pray for someone else, make sure you do so with the intention of helping them achieve their highest good. Don't do spells involving another person unless they ask you, except when there is a real danger to yourself or others. Ethical practice extends to how we represent ourselves in the world. Specifically, when we are talking to others about our practice of Modern Hekatean Witchcraft, we shouldn't try to convert them to our way of thinking nor should we belittle their beliefs. In addition, we shouldn't run around telling people how to do witchcraft or practice devotion to Hekate.

The Three Selves

Our external self is the result of the combination of our three internal selves. The lower self is the realm of emotions, while the middle self is the land of actions, and the higher self is the place of intellect. These three combined make us into the unique creations that we are.

The Lower Self

While some may perceive the Under World as a foreboding place, it is deep within our own beings that emotions dwell. You can think of our emotions as roots that extend down into the soil of the Under World pulling up the nutrients necessary to fuel both our actions and our intellect. It is our emotions that can lead us into a destructive version of the Under World – we can be anxious, depressed or suffer from significant distress. We use the metaphor of the "dark night of the soul" to describe difficult times in our lives. The primary sensation associated with these painful experiences can be found in our emotional responses. The lower self is seen as the realm of emotions. The energetic location of the lower self is from the pelvis down to the bottom of your feet. This energy extends deep roots down into the earth. We can release our pain into the ground and find rebirth.

Through this approach, we can learn to quell our fear-based emotions. The principle of passion resides in the Lower Self.

The Higher Self

At the other end is our intellect, the home of integrity. If our Lower Self energy gives us roots into the earth, then our Higher Self is our branches reaching up to the heavens. This is the realm of thoughts. Our thoughts are the one part of our human skill set that we truly have dominion over. No matter what the situation, we can change our thoughts to better manage what's going on. We can release harmful thought patterns up to the skies above to find healing. Our positive thoughts create a powerful force within ourselves and the world. The Higher Self is in the land of intellect, when we are in control of our destructive thought patterns we are naturally highly motivated to seek out knowledge and further our personal development. The energetic location for the Higher Self is the crown of our head.

The Middle Self

In between the Lower Self and the Higher Self is the Middle World self. The primary energy of the Middle Self is the action that arises from the combined energies of our intellect and emotions. The energetic core of the Middle Self is at our heart center. Thus, wisdom is gained through the activities of the Middle World self or we hurt others and our behaviors if we are being controlled by our Shadow Self. Kindness is associated with the Middle Self.

Exercise: Unifying the Three Selves Meditation

We use symbolic imagery in meditations because it helps to focus our attention on the intention of the work we are undertaking. When we focus on a symbol, we can create a channel between its energy and our own. In addition, when we quiet the mind from our everyday concerns, we open our mind to the other levels of consciousness. By consciousness, I simply mean a perceived state of being. The three main types of altered consciousness that we focus on in this book are: 1.) the soul, 2.) the energy of all things, and 3.) Hekatean energy. The soul is often blocked off from our everyday life. We want to establish a connection with our soul from the outset of our work in this book, so that's what we'll do in the meditation.

You need to be in a calm, quiet space for about 15 minutes to a half-hour. I always do meditations lying down and covered up with a blanket, but you can sit if you like! The important thing is to be comfortable and not have any parts of your body crossed. This can result in energy blockages, and it can lead to cramps. Neither of which you want.

Once you are comfortable, take three slow, deep breaths ... in ... and ... out. These should be calming breaths so don't hold it or draw it out longer than comfortable.

Close your eyes. In your mind's eye, see the number nine. Breathe in deeply, pulling it all the way down to the tips of your toes. Release. Feel your toes, feet and ankles relax.

Now see an "8", again breathe in all the way down to your toes. As you breathe out, feel the relaxation extend up through your calves to your knees.

On "7" as you exhale, your thighs and hips completely relax.

Six ... your bottom, reproductive bits and pelvis relax as you exhale.

Now on 5, your out-breath takes away all tension in your belly.

As you see the "4", envision your lungs and heart center emptying of all stress.

Three ... your throat relaxes ... the calmness of truth speaking floods in ...

Here is "2", and as you exhale, your face relaxes.

And "1" erases all tension from your mind.

Take a few more relaxing breaths. If any thoughts come up, just envision them sliding away on a cloud or down a river. You can return to them later. Don't judge those thoughts or yourself for having them. You are calm. The opening between your three selves and your soul is at your disposal. You can unify them.

Begin with your Under World self. The color of this energy is black. Let all your unwanted emotions slide down through the soles of your feet into the ground. Feel the emotions that you want to hang on to, such as kindness. Imagine the feelings you want to pull forward in your life.

Move onto your Upper World self: the realm of intellect. The color of this energy is white. Let unnecessary ways of thinking float away. Savour the knowledge that you already possess. Envision the things you hope to learn.

Turn your attention to your Middle World self. Draw down your intellectual self and draw up your emotional self so that you meet at your heart center. As the black and white energy cords come together, the color red emerges as a new energy current. All undesirable behaviors are released. Actions that move you towards a magical life are activated.

Feel all three selves unify in your heart center. Enjoy this feeling. Take a few deep, calm breaths here. The three colors mingle together and course throughout your entire being. As this is happening, you notice a fourth color, wrapping around the three cords. This is the beautiful silver of your soul. It envelops the three selves in a sheath of pure truth. Feel your unified self energy flow through every part of you. Enjoy this state of calm activation for as long as you need.

When you are ready to return to everyday consciousness, count your way back to reality …

At nine, feel your intellect turn back to everyday life, charged with the unified energy …

Now at "8," your eyes slowly open, your jaw returns to its normal position.

As "7" comes to your mind's eye, your throat is ready for speaking.

Six brings with it a resumption of your usual breathing and heart rate ...

While "5" finds the muscles in your lower torso returning to a state of calm readiness.

Four pulls this feeling down into your hips and pelvis ...

As "3" extends it down through your thighs ...

Now at "2", your calves feel energized ...

And finally, at "1" your ankles and feet return to their normal state.

When you are ready, open your eyes (if you haven't already done so). Take your time getting up. Be gentle with yourself.

Record your meditative experience in your journal. Here are some questions to help you describe your meditation:

- What images did you see?
- Did you receive any messages from your three selves or your soul?
- Were there any physical sensations?
- How do you feel now that the meditation is over?

After the meditation, you may feel sleepy or very energetic. If you are sleepy, it may be because you released excessive emotions and need to rest while the balance is restored. If you are energized, you could have been "too much in your head" and released a lot of excess thoughts. As the three selves are now unified, in a state of balance, you may feel like focusing on one aspect more than another. This is especially true if one of the three selves had been neglected. Pay attention to how you feel, think, and act in the days that follow. Writing about them in your journal is a good idea. You can do this meditation whenever you feel overwhelmed, stressed or too wound up to help return you to a balanced state.

The True Self

The three selves come together in a synergistic way to make the true self. The primary energy of the true self is love. Not the sickening sweet sort, but the dominant creative energy that drives the natural cycles of all things. When our Lower Self, Middle Self and Higher Self are working in harmony, they tap into our soul, the unborn self that's the eternal part of our being. What happens to so many of us is that we have invalidating experiences that cause our true self to go into hiding. Many of the activities in this book are designed to pull forward this true self. It is only by living as our true self can we fully become devotees of Hekate and highly effective in our witchery. However, when the true self is forced into hiding due to external circumstances such as abuse and trauma, another form of self steps in as a protector. Unfortunately, this shadow self, while protective, acts from a position of fear-based energy that can do us a great deal of harm.

The Shadow Self

Our shadow is a way of grouping together our painful experiences, harmful thoughts, fear-based emotions and our dysfunctional behaviors. The Shadow Self exists as part of each of our three selves. However, while the three selves combine in a synergistic way with our soul, the shadow self can never connect to our soul in the same manner. This is the divine energy of the soul protecting it from an invasion of fear-based energy. When we are living as our shadow self, we perceive this blockage as a sort of emptiness. That's the divine energy of our soul reaching out to prompt us towards the direction of our true self. We shouldn't try to eliminate the shadow instead we learn to control it. This course is designed to remove power from the shadow.

The Three Realms

The same basic energies at work on the individual level also function on the grand energetic scale. The primary focus of the

Under World is emotions, the key role of the Upper World is intellect, and the Middle World is the land of action. Think of it this way – the Middle World represents our everyday lives. It is the realm on which we are having this current human experience. The Upper World is the realm of higher consciousness, the place where our unborn souls eternally reside, while the Under World is the deep dive into the realm of life and death.

Under World energy is heavy and dense and that of the Upper World is light and refined. At the depths of the Under World, the experience is overwhelming because we can't see anything. We can't breathe because the air is too heavy. At the heights of the Upper World, we are overwhelmed because we can perceive everything. It's like standing on top of a mountain on a cold, clear day. It's difficult to breathe because the air is so light. Thus, in our human form, we must remain in or near the Middle World, although we can experience brief sojourns into the fringes of the other two realms. But, their depths and heights are not places for humans.

How Hekate is Involved in the Three Realms

Many of us come to Hekatean devotion already aware of Her Under World aspects. During the twentieth century, as I've previously mentioned, there was a lot of emphasis on Her as the Dark Mother, the Queen of the Under World, and the Goddess of the Witches. As the Crone, she is seen as an Under World figure. This is the reason that some of those called by Her hesitate – they are afraid of getting involved with a deity that is purely of the Under World. However, Her dark, destructive, and deadly side is only one part of Her. She is equally, if not more so, an Upper World deity. Here in the Middle World, Her energy creates our life's journey and She lights the way. I'll talk a lot about Hekate and the three worlds in Lesson Four when we cover Her many epithets. These currents combine synergistically to create the

World Soul. Using the three worlds and the epithets provide us with tools to better understand Her.

Sovereignty

Think of sovereignty as your personal declaration of independence. While we are devotees of Hekate, we are in no way subservient to Her. Quite the contrary, in fact. Our acts of devotion to Hekate are a show of our respect for Her powers and for Her guidance and intervention on our behalf. Hekate, in my experience, does not call weak lambs to her. No, it's the strong ones that She beckons. Through devotional acts, which we'll discuss more in the lesson on honoring Hekate, we not only respect Our Lady but also re-affirm our commitment to our own personal development. Hekate is both external to us and within us. When we honor Her, we are engaging in intentional self-respect because it affirms the divine within each of us. While devotion is in our own best interests, communing with Hekate through ritual or petitioning for Her intervention in our workings requires us to transcend the boundaries of usual human existence. Witchcraft requires us to manipulate the natural energies around us and enter altered states of consciousness. There are times when, in an altered state, we travel to the energetic realms. Moreover, when working with herbs, stones or other correspondences or with Hekate, we summon our own internal magic and blend it with external forces. When we engage in metaphysical activities, such as divination or spiritual journeying, we enter an altered state of consciousness. Learning to maintain our sovereignty during these activities is perhaps the most important aspect of witchcraft. This is especially true for those who have great innate magical abilities. In my experience, Hekate often calls such people. It's vital that we learn to control our personal state of being to maintain sovereignty during and after workings. Just like in everyday life, we need boundaries or else we risk getting swept away on the energies that we summon and the metaphysical spaces we enter.

Another threat to our sovereignty comes from the energy of

other people. Witches are often highly empathic, so that we easily pick up on how others feel. We also often have a natural tendency to want to heal others because we can feel their suffering. Being empathic is a true blessing, but we can't walk through life soaking up everyone's energy. Plus, unless we're asked for help, it's none of our business. The same techniques that we employ to maintain sovereignty when we make magic can also be applied to maintaining our boundaries with others. In addition, developing these skills help when we get overwhelmed by our own energies. Those times when we are stressed, wound-up or spiralling with our thoughts. As witches, we have an abundance of natural energies – emotional, cognitive and behavioral – that we can learn to control and use for our own best interests. Living a magical life helps to focus our energy overall, but there are certain skills that can really train us to be better at managing our internal forces. There are simple techniques that we can learn that help us manage our magical connections, enforce personal boundaries and become better at controlling our internal states, thereby ensuring our personal sovereignty.

Balancing, Centering and Grounding

There are three different types of techniques that help maintain our individual sovereignty. Balancing refers to the practice of maintaining and restoring a sense of calm awareness that is necessary for effective witchcraft. Centering is about standing in our own physical power. For the times we feel disconnected from the world, too enmeshed with the metaphysical or sucked into others' energies, we can use grounding to correct the situation.

Balancing

Being balanced means that we have an internal equilibrium that is known to us and that we can return to at will. A regular meditation practice is the best way to become more balanced in general. Meditation develops our mind so that we can quickly return to a balanced state when out-of-whack. Self-reflection helps us to determine what this equilibrium means to us. Although the principles are designed to help you live a more balanced life, how you interpret and apply them is very much up to you. Balance is the same – what would be chaotic for one person is calm for the other. I encourage you to embark on your own journey of discovering what balance means to you.

While balance overall is a complex process requiring self-study and continual review, the technique of balancing our energies is simple. There are many ways of accomplishing a balanced energetic state, but the basic premise of them all is to create a state of calm awareness. Meditation that seeks to quiet the mind is a great way to master this. However, the first step is to develop an automatic self check-in process. This is vital prior and after any magical working, but also is so beneficial in our everyday lives.

Self Check-In

As witches, we want to develop our ability to be automatically aware of our internal states, thoughts and feelings. The only rule of witchcraft that really matters is "know thyself." Through knowing what's going on inside of us, we can learn to manage these things and then apply these skills to the way we manipulate external energetic forces. Sounds so simple, but in practice it's loads of work. Totally worth it, though. A simple self check-in practice consisting of regularly pausing for a few moments before beginning any new activity helps. Ask yourself:

- How am I feeling? Am I hungry? Tired? In pain?
- What am I thinking? Are my thoughts swirling?
- What do I need to accomplish this next activity?
- Is this in my own best interest? If not, how I can make it so?

Adding these practices to your Witch's Hour of Power is a great way to get in the habit of doing the balance check-in. One more thought – when I say "calm but aware" I am not talking about being some sort of Zen-zombie. Not at all. Recall that passion is one of our principles. Calm awareness is about being in control of our passion, rather than it running our lives. Passion without proper care and attention can become unruly.

Grounding

Grounding is a technique for connecting ourselves to the present moment. If you're feeling disconnected from your surroundings or your own internal states, too involved with others' problems, buzzing from energy in the natural environment or generally stressed out, grounding yourself is quite helpful. We also need to ground ourselves before and after doing magic. Prior to workings, getting grounded helps us to remove any of the things mentioned earlier. Afterwards, it returns us to the Middle World, so we can get on with our everyday lives.

The simplest form of grounding consists of focusing on different parts of the physical environment. Whenever you are feeling overwhelmed or disconnected from reality (whether after a working or in everyday life), pull yourself back to your body by asking and answering these questions:

What is one thing I can see?
What is one thing I can smell?
What is one thing I can feel?
What is one thing I can hear?

Develop a detailed description in your mind's eye for each question, as though you were doing so for a friend on the phone. I recommend practicing this technique when you aren't feeling wonky so that you're comfortable doing it when you are having difficulty coming back "down to earth" after a working. Like the self check-in, grounding only takes a few moments and can be added to your Witch's Hour of Power as part of your daily practice.

Practice: Balancing and Grounding

The sections on balancing and grounding contain techniques that will help you develop your witchery by increasing your ability to control your emotional and cognitive states. Everything is energy, and our feelings and thoughts are no exception. It's a good idea to practice the skills discussed in the last two sections and then record your answers to the questions in your journal.

Next Level Grounding

Sometimes you may need a more intense grounding technique if you're really soaring high after a metaphysical experience or dealing with a lot of stress or horrible people. It's helpful to take several deep breaths then envision yourself as a tree. Your feet connect to the earth beneath you, releasing all the excess emotional energy down into the ground where it will be reborn anew. Envision that your thought overload is releasing up to the heavens where it will also be recycled into something of value. As you release these unnecessary feelings and thoughts, envision pulling in calming energy from both sources.

Centering

Centering helps us to achieve the state of calm awareness using our physical being. I use centering often because I tend to get completely up in my head, ignoring everything below my neck. Not only do I get more stressed when I do this, I tend to ignore basic bodily needs like eating and going to the bathroom! Being centered is a core skill for magic as well. When we create intentional awareness of our own physical state, the benefits are many, including:

- Increased consciousness of our bodily needs
- Naturally diminished desire to do harmful things to our bodies
- Awareness of the power of our bodies
- Connection to this power to use in magic

Exercise: Centering

Stand with your feet hip-width apart. Your arms should be relaxed at your sides, with your gaze straight ahead, fixed on one point. Turn your attention to your feet. Is there tension in them? Relax them and spread your toes. Evenly distribute your weight between the balls of your feet and your heels. Bring your attention up through your calves to your knees. Again, check for tension and release it, slightly relaxing your knees. Continue with this up to your trunk. At your heart center envision a cord running through your body down into the earth and up to the sky. Is this cord straight? Correct your posture as necessary to straighten it out. Continue with the relaxing technique up through your shoulders, neck and down into your finger tips. Then pull that calm awareness up to meet the same in your mind. When doing any sort of working, you should start by ensuring that you are centered by checking in with this cord. Of course, you need to be balanced and grounded as well. When your working is complete, do the grounding if required and check-in with that cord.

Spiritual Upgrades

I find that balancing, centering and grounding are especially important for me when I am receiving a spiritual upgrade. What I mean by this are the times when my understanding of metaphysical forces – and myself – goes through an intense period of change. One way to look at this is using the idea of energetic vibration. A spiritual upgrade is when our vibration changes. We become better at various aspects of witchcraft, such as being able to connect with Hekate, conjure energy or our psychic abilities quickly improve. Doing the exercises in the course will create the perfect condition for such an upgrade to occur. During these times, it can be difficult for me to keep my feet on the ground because my mind is being so rapidly expanded. This might happen to you during this course. If you start to feel disconnected from reality, use the techniques to keep yourself in this world. Let the upgrade happen but manage it wisely. Journaling is also quite helpful.

The Witch's Mind

It's our witch's mind that enables a spiritual upgrade to occur. Our mind is the greatest magical tool we have. We are hardwired with certain attributes that render us more open to the various types of energetic forces. These characteristics include curiosity and powerful observation skills. Keeping our curiosity alive is a vital part of witchcraft. Desiring to understand more and looking for the answers motivates us. Being a natural observer lets us step back from things to determine what's really going on. Because we are curious observers, we are always open to inspiration. Without inspiration we lose the ability to develop spells, write rituals and manipulate energy. Journaling about what you want to know more about is a great tactic. If you're not feeling curious, start by noticing all the thoughts you have during the day. Ask yourself "why?" and then go from there. Our witch's mind is the thing that compels us to live a magical life; it's what tells us that there is something more. That's the key to a magical life, the passion for seeking more, the kindness to achieve the life with grace and compassion for others and the integrity to act in a responsible way.

Solitary Practice

This course is designed for the solitary practitioner. You may not have the support of others while you undergo the spiritual upgrade that is this course. As an individual working with metaphysical forces – and your own actions, feelings and thoughts – it's crucial that you maintain your sovereignty. There is a temptation to loosen our boundaries and ignore what's in our own best interests when we are learning about witchcraft. This is because we want to truly understand the mysteries. In addition, we often genuinely want to help others. Without a mentor and community to check-up on you, it's even more important to use the balancing, centering and grounding techniques so that you are acting as your own supervisor. Extending this idea, you are also your own High Priestess or Priest. At the end of this course, you can elect to perform self-initiation which means that you are formally acknowledging yourself as such – your own minister, advisor and magical coach.

Summary

This course outlines the basic concepts of the Keeping Her Keys perspective that you can adapt in a way that makes sense to you. Living a magical life includes kindness, integrity and passion. These principles are represented in the three worlds of the self. The Under World self is the realm of emotions, while the Upper World is the plane of the intellect. The Middle World is the land of actions born from the combination of intellect and emotions. These three worlds exist on the grand scale as well and provide us with a way of understanding Hekate's energy. We help to manage our sovereignty through meditation and other techniques including balancing, centering and grounding. These practices are often necessary to help us deal with our innate witchiness and are especially important when we are undergoing spiritual upgrades. The Witch's Mind is our most powerful tool we have, so taking great care of it is a must. Taking great care of ourselves is particularly important since many of us practicing Hekate's Modern Witchcraft are solitary witches.

Lesson 3: Working with Hekate

Hekate came to me when I was at my weakest. You may be reading this because She did the same for you. Since Hekate called me, She has become my guide, my protector and my intervenor. When I am troubled, I turn to Her and find solace. She has always accepted me for who I am, although She is quick to kick my ass if I am out of line. As I walk this journey, I've learned so much about Her, witchcraft, and how to live my truth. I don't always feel close to Her, but I know She is as near as my cry of "Help me." Although I have a close relationship with Hekate, I am not in any way consumed by Her. I am an independent person, with free will to do as I please. In my personal perspective, I believe that the more I try to live a magical life, study, practice witchcraft and work on myself, the closer I become to Hekate. Through self-development, I have become better at connecting with Her, both through direct and indirect communication routes.

Like any relationship, mine with Hekate changes over time. In the beginning, I was timid of Her, mainly because of my limited understanding. There have been times when I have resisted Her since then, especially when I know that I am not exactly living a magical life. I've pulled back from Her, and at times it's felt as though She's walked away from me. Through it all, there is an unbreakable cord connecting me to Her. I've developed a close connection that enables me to tap into Her energy – if not get Her actual attention – quickly and effectively. As our relationship has deepened, my own motivation to live a magical life has steadily increased. She's been my guide through my own personal Under World that I've written about in the Keeping Her Keys blog. There's been times that Hekate seems to stand directly before me, demanding that I must do a particular thing. For example, when She came to me with the idea to start the blog, that grew into a movement, and then into this book. If there's one thing above every other lesson that I've learned on my journey with Hekate is that I need to have faith. This has been so difficult for me! But, faith is required for developing a close relationship with Our Lady. We must believe in Her and trust in Her. More importantly, we must have faith in ourselves.

Establishing a Relationship

A leap of faith is required when Hekate first calls you. It's that simple. You may have existing ideas about Our Lady. You may already have a working relationship with another deity. You may not really believe in Hekate. That's all fine. However, if She is calling you, and you've gotten this far in the book, then chances are that you are interested in establishing a relationship with Hekate. Much of this book is dedicated to helping you establish a relationship with Hekate. You'll learn Her many names (Lesson 4), Her symbols (Lesson 8), and Her correspondences (Lesson 9). Through learning about these things, you'll develop a better understanding of Hekate. Each time we learn something new, we add a bit of Hekate's energy into our own. This is part of how we complete Hekate. We also complete Her through the energy we create in our acts of devotion. There's a detailed description of honoring Hekate in Lesson 6. She completes us by protecting us, guiding us, and giving us the keys of our lives. There are so many mutual benefits in our relationship with Hekate. However, we need to be mindful of establishing a healthy relationship. Being sincere in our devotion and trying to live a magical life will help get this relationship off to a good start. Whether we are just forming our relationship with Hekate, or we've been a devotee for ages, the most important part of any relationship, including ours with Hekate, is good communication.

The Central Role of Communication

Communication between us and Hekate is the most important part of our relationship with Her. Hekate speaks to us and we do the same in return. We need to be specific and clear about what we want. Moreover, we need to learn how to understand Hekate's communications with us.

How We Communicate with Hekate

There are many ways that we can communicate with Hekate. We can communicate with Her directly through chants, prayers, songs and written words. You've already experienced the power of praying to Hekate. I suggest that you write your own prayers to Her. Early in your relationship with Our Lady, your prayers are a way of establishing an initial connection with Hekate. By speaking the words of the prayers in this book, you are opening an energy current with Her. At times, this is a gentle wave hello. As you progress in your relationship, and work through this book, that way will gradually become a conversation. Accompanying this increased dialogue will be a greater connection to Her energy. At times, you will experience direct communication with Hekate herself rather than only accessing Her energy currents. This can be achieved either with Hekate as all that She is, or with one aspect of Her. When this happens, you'll have a transformative experience.

There are other ways that we use words to talk to Hekate, such as through chants, rituals, and spells. We use techniques such as evocation when we really want to get Her attention. These communication techniques all rely on words. We also communicate with Hekate through the act of writing, which is why it's so important that we develop our own prayers, chants, rituals, and spells. We can also write poems and stories about Hekate and our relationship with Her as a way of indirectly communicating with Her. Any time we put words out there that honor Her, She receives them. There is a deeper form of communication with Hekate known as communion. This is when we directly connect to Hekate, when we transcend accessing Her through energy currents and stand fully in Her presence.

Such moments are achieved through study, practice, and living a magical life. When we are in communion with Hekate, we can also directly feel Her presence without the need for words. It is a profound experience.

Equally important to the things we say to Hekate is our ability to listen to Her. Listening is a necessary skill in any healthy relationship, ours with Hekate is no different. Being a good listener means that you will keep an energy channel between you and Her open always. You've created this initial channel by doing the ritual in the first Lesson and the meditation at the end of the second one. Think of this as your personal phone with Hekate. She can call anytime; you just have to pick up. Contrast this to not having a phone – you'd miss Her call. It's important to manage this connection. You don't want to be keeping Her always on the phone, you just want Her there, and you want to be available for when She contacts you. In my experience, Hekate most often speaks to us in a calm, clear voice. Since She is all-powerful, She doesn't need to yell. Moreover, Hekate doesn't usually raise Her voice, unless the situation is dire. You must be listening to hear Her. Again, we're back to the idea that we are sovereign beings. If we don't care to listen, She is not going to continue. However, there are times when we will hear Her loud and clear. The initial call from Her is often like this, as are times when our lives are veering dangerously off course. These instances are infrequent – unless, of course, your life is a hot mess. In that case, you're not listening to Her at all because She'll give you're the advice you need to get out of any situation. You may think that listening refers to receiving auditory messages from Hekate, but there's much more to listen for. Pay attention to the symbols She sends, the people in your life, and your own internal voice.

Hekate's Ways of Communicating

In addition to direct communication and sending symbols,

there are other ways that Hekate chooses to connect with us. Often, it can just be a feeling we have that She is watching over us. Although there are countless other ways that Hekate communicates with us, I've listed some of the more common ones below.

Signs

Hekate often speaks to us through Her symbols. We'll review Her symbols and correspondences in future lessons. Start looking around for unexpected examples. Be on the lookout for random keys showing up in your life already since you've already made the commitment to this course. Other signs often include spontaneous encounters with dogs – especially black ones – that are totally out of sync with what you're doing. There will also be signs that are magical only to you.

Dreams

Another way Hekate speaks to us is in our dreams. This is because our busy minds are quieted by sleep, allowing our established connection with Our Lady to flow more freely. While She may come to you as Herself in a dream, She may also use signs in dreams. She could even appear in a human form that's quite unexpected. Hekate will take on whatever form is most appropriate for getting Her point across and for getting your attention. Keeping a dream journal is a good practice to establish. Through writing about your dreams, you will notice things that you would otherwise miss.

Meditations

Thinking back on the Unifying the Three Selves Meditation, recall the state of calm openness that you achieved. In this altered consciousness, we are more open to receive direct messages from Hekate. These messages can be audible – like a whisper – or they can appear as written text on your mind's eye. She may even appear to you and say things. Symbols may also appear during your meditations. That's why it's important to meditate as you develop your relationship with Her. Each time you enter this altered state, you strengthen that energetic connection with Her. However, you need to pace yourself. Meditating in the hope of receiving direct communication from Hekate too often can be exhausting and ineffective.

Direct Messages

Hekate may directly communicate with you during chanting, praying, acts of devotion, or when you are doing a spell. That's in addition to the methods I've listed above – through dreams and in meditations. I want to mention one last type of direct communication, what I call the instant download. This happens when you are going about your regular life and suddenly She speaks to you. This can take the form of a vision, you can hear Her speak, or a message may suddenly flash across your mind's eye. When this happens, it can be quite startling. It can also be difficult to write about it immediately after since you may be doing something else – like the laundry. Do your best to journal your experience as soon as you can.

Events

There are times when Hekate speaks to us through events in our lives. I've heard so many stories where Hekate comes forward for the first time when a person is at their lowest. By turning to Hekate – and using Her energy – to learn from our disasters, She speaks to us through these calamities. Another way She can speak to us through an event occurs when a scenario plays out that is so unusual that the entire situation seems to be a message from Lady Hekate. For example, I know someone who unexpectedly altered her morning route because she was late. On this different way to work, she found a heart-shaped key with "you are loved" engraved on it. At the time she was going through a very difficult time in her personal life and was feeling quite unloved. No one came forward to claim the key. This is an example of an entire event being a message.

Inner Knowing

There are times when we just know something. There's no other explanation. For me, this often happens when I wake up in the morning. One way of looking at this is that it is our intuition talking, while another is that this is a message that flowed through our established energy channel with Hekate. It's like when you look at someone and instantly know what they are thinking. Typically, the inner knowing accompanies one of the other types of messages, but there are times when we just *know* without any other evidence.

Hearing Hekate's Voice for the First Time

The first time Hekate communicates with us can be a surprising, and even frightening, experience for people. Perhaps you've purchased this book because you felt called by Hekate but weren't sure what to do. Sometimes people are afraid of Hekate's calling. They've heard a bit about Her – maybe that She's the Dark Mother or Queen of the Witches. Perhaps they are content with their established spiritual practice (or lack thereof). They might not have a clue who She is or what is going on. Typically, She persists with complete disregard for personal resistance or ignorance. Up until a point, and then She will retreat. While you retain your sovereignty, She cannot be manipulated.

Part of that departure from a more mainstream pagan form of relationship with deity is that She expects certain things from Her followers. There isn't a how-to manual on how to practice devotion, but there are ancient scripts and modern gnosis. My belief, and that of many others, is that skepticism is one of the principles expected of Her devotees. If you're feeling called by Hekate, take the time to critically evaluate the situation. She doesn't want blind acceptance. She requires conscious devotion.

Oftentimes, Hekate summons us with the intensity of a religious conversion (since that is basically what's going on). Afterward, we must contemplate the calling before going forward. If we find ourselves unprepared or unwilling, then we need to have a well thought out answer when we reject Her. If we walk blindly into devotion, then we are being ignorant, and She is likely to reject us, having found us unworthy. If you aren't ready for devotion right now, perhaps you can make an agreement with Her to delay things for a while. She may agree to it. If you're hesitating, figure out why.

Understanding: Noticing Hekate's Signs

Use your intuition to determine if a thought or image that occurs to you is a sign from Hekate. Do the same with your external surroundings. If you practice this for a couple of weeks, you'll really strengthen your awareness of Hekate. Once it's an established habit, you'll do it automatically. I'm asking you to use your intuition for interpreting whether something is a sign rather than referring to sources because this intuition is vital for becoming a powerful witch. It's our own innate wisdom and is very valuable for devotion, witchery, and personal development work.

Seeking Hekate

There are times when we truly need to establish direct communication with Hekate, when we really need her guidance, intervention or protection. A dear friend of mine and I call these "bathroom" moments. This refers to times when we've found ourselves on our knees in public bathrooms, crying out for Hekate's assistance. I think this all got started several years ago when I desperately needed a new car. I was going through a divorce and had lost just about everything, including my minivan, except my two sons. I was driving the old clunker that my older son owned. It was beyond repair, so I set off to buy a used car at a dealership about an hour from my place. Then there were complications because my child support was not court ordered, so the bank wouldn't give me the financing. I refused to be defeated. Out of desperation, I dropped to my knees in the car dealership and petitioned Hekate for Her help. Miraculously, I walked out of there with a brand-new car with 0.0% financing. There is no logical explanation for this – I wasn't working, and my credit was in the toilet due to the divorce. Hekate prevailed! The bathroom moment was born.

Here's a less dramatic example of seeking Hekate's help. Quite a few years ago, shortly after that bathroom moment – I found myself wondering around a big bookstore, bereft and desperate for ... something, anything to make the pain go away. I was completely exhausted – from a broken heart, too much drama and the complex series of life changes resulting from the ending of a romantic relationship. Silently, I prayed to Hekate to show me the way to relief from my distress. I turned a corner and found a great self-help book (that had nothing to do with Our Lady). That book helped me through that dark night of my soul.

However, there are times when I am seeking Her that She appears distant or even silent. My prayers, rituals, meditative journeys all lead to anywhere but Her. Or so it seems. I've learned over the years that when She seems absent, She is present, but I'm not listening.

Hekate is Everywhere

Before I can get to the place where I can listen to Hekate, I need to find Her. Using Her symbols – like keys, torches, snakes – helps to focus attention on connecting to Hekate. Sometimes these symbols – including black dogs – show up unannounced indicating that She is close to us. Other times, connecting to the energy of the symbol provides a conduit for direct communion with Our Lady. I see Her in all aspects of everyday life, especially the natural world – from the rose bushes to the waves on the ocean. There are so many opportunities to meditate on Her creation as a means of connecting to Her.

Focusing on Hekate

Some simple examples of using natural energies to focus petitioning for Hekate's presence include making an offering of natural things such as roses or garlic, standing at a liminal space, or contemplating the starry sky on the Dark Moon. We'll be discussing these activities throughout the book. Adding your own prayer for connecting is important. One thing I've found is that Hekate appreciates effort, which is why I think it's vital to worship Her through creating your own prayers. You be the judge of what's appropriate in any situation.

But, She's Also Nowhere

There is a problem with the fact that She is everywhere – She can also seem to be nowhere. She can be elusive. I've learned that this is mostly selfishness on my part. It's not Hekate's mission to appear on command, but rather it's my work to find Her where She is.

It's Not Her, It's Me

If I can't connect to Hekate, I've learned that it's something about me that is the block. To put it shortly: It's not Her, it's me. Sometimes, I am determined to manifest something that clearly is not in my own best interest. She'll answer by ignoring my pleas. Other times, I need to sort things out on my own instead of asking Her for a miracle. I've learned that seeking Her guidance is the surest way to find Her, while asking for stuff is a guarantee of being denied access to Her favor.

Establishing a Meaningful Connection

There are several factors involved in establishing a meaningful connection with Hekate, including knowing what we want and being well-informed.

Determine the Goal

The first step in connecting with Hekate is to be clear about your desired outcome when you find Her. I'm going to divide goals into two broad categories: finding Her for the first time and connecting with Her after you've become a devotee. If you are seeking Hekate to establish an initial connection, then you need to ask yourself if you are prepared to be a devotee. If you're interested in a casual working relationship where She grants your wishes and you do nothing in return, save yourself the time and effort. Determine what you hope to get out of the relationship if you're new to devotion or why you are seeking communion if you are already a devotee. Communion simply means an intense episode of connection.

Being Better

For me, as an initiate, I wanted to be better. Just that – better in all areas of my life from the most mundane tasks to my witchcraft. I've noticed that this general desire, if it is sincere, is enough to light the torch that leads to Her. It's also true that Hekate often calls to us when we are at our most desperate. We must be open to receiving Her. When we are at our weakest, our ego defenses get broken down and we become open to that connection.

Be Wary of the Shadow Block

However, sometimes when we are looking for Her it is really our ego trying to get what it wants. She knows the difference. Another scenario occurs when our higher self is seeking Her because it knows that we are in trouble, but our shadow self is dominant, so we get blocked from connecting. I think it's important to tap into our higher selves as a means of figuring out what our goal is and as an aid for guiding us to Hekate.

Be Informed

Ask questions, read books and learn the ancient texts. If you are new to Hekate, cast your net broadly and read a variety of books. I've noticed that many people still view Her primarily as an Under World goddess or Queen of the Witches. These roles are a very small part of Hekate, as you'll read in Lesson 4.

I hope these tips help you when with your efforts to communicate with Hekate. Be patient with yourself – and Her – if you experience difficulties.

Interpreting Hekate's Messages

Another potentially challenging area besides trying to connect with Hekate is in making sense of the messages you receive. I've previously mentioned the two most important things – listening and writing things down. By listening, I'm talking about observing both your internal world and the external one. Pay attention. Once you receive a message, write about it in as much detail as you need to make sense of it. If you're pressed for time, jot down a few key points or make a quick recording on your device. You can use these prompts to write about the message in more detail later. Of course, there are times when the message is so vivid that there's no way you could possibly forget it. Don't forget to write about these times, too. You may be able to find a deeper meaning through your description of the event. After you write about the event, you need to then contemplate the message. While it's a great idea to refer to books about the meaning of things, it's better to rely on your own interpretation before seeking out secondary sources.

Applying Hekate's Messages in Your Life

After you've processed the message, the next – and most vital –

step is to determine how to use the information She's given you. Sometimes, this can be obvious because we've received either a spoken or written message that's perfectly clear. Then there are the times that Hekate communicates through actions, like in my car and bookstore examples. However, there will also be times when how you should apply Her message is not that clear. It can also be that the message is clear, but what you're being guided to do seems difficult or even ridiculous. I've learned to trust in my ability to correctly interpret Hekate's messages, and you should, too. You'll know when you've received a genuine message. And if you get a message, don't you owe it to Hekate to at least try to apply it? However, if the application – or even the meaning – of the message is unclear to you or seems beyond realization – go back to Hekate and seek further guidance. Don't be afraid to ask Her for help.

Processing an Encounter with Hekate

The questions below are easily adaptable for use when processing just about anything. In your journal, answer these questions in relation to your first encounter with Hekate:

How did Hekate appear to you?

Although the first encounter with Hekate is something that most people can't forget, it makes sense to think about and record how She appears to you: what symbols are present? What else is in the vision? What type of vision is it (auditory, visual)? Was there a real-life display? Get it all down before you start researching things. I think your personal representation of this vision is far better than what you'll read anywhere.

What did She want?

Hekate comes to us when She feels that we can serve Her well. She has something in mind. If there isn't clear information about the specifics, spend some time in contemplation analyzing the contents of the calling. Trust me, She's not as ambiguous as She initially appears. Is She calling you to a long-term relationship or a short-term association? I'm wary of thinking that She wants a fling with anyone, but it is possible.

What did I already know about Hekate?

When I was called, I was resistant. What I knew of Hekate was the mainstream pagan version as a dark goddess. At the time, I was a member of the Fellowship of Isis and a big fan of Artemis. Devotion has been vastly different than being a fan girl. Take some time to record your ideas and knowledge. Don't go poking around the internet too much before doing this. It's important to record what you already know.

What was my mindset? What were my dominant feelings?

If there's one thing I know for sure about being a devotee, is that She demands we have our emotional and cognitive act together. However, She often calls us at our most desperate. Are you depressed, anxious and/or distressed? Are you harbouring harmful thoughts including resentments, grudges, or bitterness? A magical life is one of constant, conscious self-improvement.

Summary

At the heart of Hekate's Modern Witchcraft is Her connection with each practitioner. This relationship is based on effective communication between you and Our Lady. There are several ways that you can communicate with Hekate. You can directly petition Her through speaking the words of a prayer or chant. An example of indirect communication is when we use one of Her symbols as a representation of our devotion. Just like in any relationship, it's important that we are good listeners. We accomplish this by maintaining energetic contact with Hekate and through developing our devotional practices. Hekate can choose to communicate with us in both direct and indirect ways, too. She may directly appear to us in a vision or come to us in a dream. The highest form of communication with Hekate is when communion takes place. In this altered state, it is possible to transmit messages to Her purely through our energy – especially our emotions. She will reciprocate. For many of us, Hekate calls us for the first time when we are at our weakest. However, there are other times when it can be difficult for us to get in touch with Her. When we receive messages, it's important to interpret them and then apply them in your life. Processing our encounters with Hekate helps us to decode Her messages and to better understand ourselves.

Lesson 4: Hekate and Her Many Names

The Goddess Hekate is both complex and very simple. She has many specific and diverse abilities but is also the source of pure energy. She is ancient and contemporary. I know her by a multitude of names, ranging from World Soul to Queen of the Witches. I understand her as the Keeper of the Keys of the Universe. Symbolically, her hands hold all that there is. Through my efforts, I can attain one of her many keys. I've been a devotee of Hekate for over a decade. During this time, my understanding of Hekate has grown both on the intellectual and personal levels. In my experience, her energy is intimidating but approachable. Knowing Hekate is often a very intimate experience, seldom fleeting and frequently intense. People have diverse beliefs about Hekate. And she changes with the times. However, most of my intellectual knowledge about Hekate comes from ancient sources.

Understanding: Your Hekate

Before we start discussing the various existing interpretations of Hekate, it's important for you to record your own personal vision of Hekate. When you processed your first encounter with her, you wrote about your initial impressions of her. These may have changed since then. Writing about your understanding of Hekate at this point will provide you with a reference point for how your understanding may have already changed. You can also refer to it as you go through this course.

Historical Hekate

The origins of Hekate lie in the mists of the distant past. The most likely beginning of Hekate was in Asia Minor and parts of Eastern Europe. From these regions, her cult spread to Ancient Greece where she was viewed as a Titan. Different from the rest of her Titanic pantheon, she wasn't killed by the upstart Olympians. Instead Zeus gave her dominion over land, sea and sky, according to Hesiod's *Theogony*[2] (approximately eighth century BCE). The Ancient Greeks worshiped Hekate in various ways, notably she was a matron watching over households. It is from this role that the common contemporary practice of giving her offerings on the Dark Moon[3] grew. In ancient Greece, a Hekate's Supper was left out, usually at a three-way crossroads, to seek her favor over a household for the coming month. Her association with the number three extended to her being viewed as a triple goddess.

Torch Bearing Goddess of the Under World

During this time, her image as a goddess of the Under World was also born. In the Homeric Hymn to Demeter,[4] Hekate answers Persephone's cries when no one else does. She becomes Persephone's guide between the Under World[5] and the human one, using her torches[6] to light the way along the journey. Hekate as a torch-bearer or lamp-carrier became one of the dominant themes of her depictions during ancient times.

Keeper of the Keys

During this time, the Orphic Hymn to Hekate[7] was written, as well. In this poem, Hekate is given many responsibilities, including being the universal key holder.[8]

Ancient Hekate's Many Roles

From the ancient sources, we know that Hekate was a liminal goddess, standing between worlds, particularly at the threshold of life and death. She was described in many diverse ways including Mother of All, Queen, Savior and World Soul. She was viewed as the torch-bearing guide for those on nightmarish Under World journeys. Not only was she viewed as the guide along the road, but also as the way itself. The variety of the titles bestowed upon her by the ancients often appears contradictory. We need to consider two things. One is that the ancient writers held vastly divergent views of Hekate. The other is that Hekate has always been a complex goddess with multiple roles and abilities.

The Importance of Ancient Hekate

While we will never know for certain the extend of her adoration among the ancient Greeks, there is evidence suggesting that she was an important goddess, particularly with common people. In addition, there are many ancient coins, statues, and other works of art depicting Hekate during this period.

Writings about Ancient Hekate

The Greek Magical Papyri (PGM),[9] an ancient text combining Greek, Roman and Egyptian deities, portrays Hekate as an all-purpose goddess. In many spells, she is addressed as everything from the bringer of beginnings to the mistress of corpses. In the PGM she is a goddess of the moon. There are other sources of evidence indicating that she was seen by some as a triple-moon goddess. The Hekate of The Chaldean Oracles, written after the earlier texts, is a complex entity seen as the World Soul. As such, she acts as a sort of protective membrane between the human world and the realms. She is seen as a savior who helps human souls ascend. This is the Hekate of the ancient world. You can sort through the translations of The Greek Magical Papyri or The Chaldean Oracles yourself to learn more. Sorita d'Este's book Circle for Hekate[10] provides a great summary of historical Hekate.

The Problem with the Ancient Sources

We are fortunate to have such a large resource of ancient images and texts about Hekate. The problem with having so many ancient sources is that we can be fooled into thinking that this gives us a full understanding of how she was viewed by the ancients. Even with everything that is known, it's still impossible to piece together who Hekate truly was to the ancients. Moreover, because the texts were written by men of a certain class, there is no way to know for certain how ancient witches understood and experienced Hekate. Even with the stories about Hekate and specific witches, such as Circe, Medea[11] and Simaitha,[12] we are limited in our knowledge by the fact that these are far from factual portrayals of how the ancients may have used Hekate in witchcraft. *The Greek Magical Papyri* only provides insight into what we know refer to as ceremonial magic.

Historical Hekate: The Middle Ages – Nineteenth Century

Hekate during the Middle Ages, through the Renaissance and into the twentieth century underwent a striking narrowing of her abilities. While the ancients revered her as a goddess with many characteristics and abilities, the image that emerged afterwards is limited to that of an Under World goddess. One example of this restricted view of Hekate is found in Pistis Sophia[13] where she is portrayed as basically the Queen of Hell. Shakespeare's portrayal of her in MacBeth[14] epitomized this version of Hekate. While artists and authors presented a narrow version of Hekate and witches, it is unlikely that this reflected how witches understood and experienced Hekate during these times.

Twentieth-Century Hekate

In the early twentieth century Hekate's limited capacity as an Under World goddess was further reinforced through the works of Aleister Crowley[15] and Gerald Gardner.[16] Hekate (usually spelled the Latin way: Hecate) became widely known as the Goddess of Witchcraft in neo-pagan circles. The idea of Hekate as a crone, first advanced in *The White* Goddess,[17] spread to become a commonly held belief among neo-pagans. Within this interpretation, she was also in the "Maiden Mother Crone" tripartite goddess structure as the crone. Sometimes she is also seen as all three goddesses within the trio. There is some ancient historical evidence connecting Hekate to the Maiden Mother Crone model. In one instance, She is called the moon in its three phases. Hence the modern moon phase representation of the triple goddess. In another citation, Hekate is equated to the moon, Proserpina (Persephone) to the Under World and Diana to the earth.[18] There is ancient evidence that solidifies her as a maiden. Her role as a mother is reinforced through ancient epithets, such as *Pammetor*, and there are a few tales portraying her as a maternal figure. Thus, the twentieth-century common understanding of Hekate was limited to two roles. As part of the Triple Goddess imagery she was often celebrated as the wise woman. In her dark goddess incarnation, she could be given homage as Queen of the Witches and invoked for certain types of witchcraft.

Contemporary Hekate

Today, many Hekatean witches view Her as an all-purpose goddess. This understanding of Hekate was greatly informed by the scholarship about her ancient origins that occurred in the late twentieth century, notably S. I. Johnston's *Hekate Soteira*.[19] As the twenty-first century began, other writers were presenting alternative ideas about Hekate, too. The popular contemporary perspectives on Hekate can be divided into four distinct categories: the soul of the world, as a primordial force, as a dark goddess and as the triple goddess/crone. Sometimes Hekate is the focus of a certain path, but other times she is part of a framework rather than the focus. Some of these perspectives are more intellectual and theurgical, while others are more witchcraft based. What these approaches have in common is that Hekate is a mighty goddess and that she is a powerful magical force available to practitioners. Another shared thread is that all these perspectives use the historical interpretations of Hekate in developing their understanding.

Defining Contemporary Hekate

An important consideration when defining contemporary Hekate is that some of the approaches utilize one aspect of Hekate rather than the multitude of characteristics. My personal view is that Hekate is the energy current in all living things. My personal Hekate has always been The Dark Mother. I see all these perspectives as valid, whether they reflect my personal view because all things flow from Hekate as the source, we can use one current, say in understanding her as a dark goddess, or many as in the World Soul perspective. Another distinction is that some of these modern perspectives vary in their approach to Hekate, with some seeing her as a deity that must be petitioned for favors and others viewing her as a force that can be manipulated.

Hekate's Major Roles

There are two major ways that Hekate is viewed based on the ancient texts. The first I've already mentioned – that of the World Soul. The second is as a Dark Goddess. The World Soul is the highest representation of Hekate in the Upper World while the Goddess of the Under World shows us that She is present in the depths of suffering as well.

Hekate: The Dark and Light Mother of All

Hekate as the Dark Mother is a powerful form that She shares with many other female deities. However, I did an analysis of her many epithets based largely on the excellent database compiled by Sara Croft. This is such a rich resource that I urge you to discover it on your own (nehetisingsforhekate.tumblr. com). I used the codes of "dark," "light," and "neither." Out of all the ancient epithets on my list, I coded 20% as "dark," 24%

as "light," and the remaining 56% were "neutral." According to this analysis, Hekate is more Upper World energy than Under World. I did this analysis to illustrate that the ancients saw Hekate as more than a dark goddess. She embodies both light and dark, like magic and every one of us.

World Soul

The image of Hekate as the World Soul is as the Great Mother and Savior. In *The Chaldean Oracles* Hekate is declared as the World Soul, the vital force that fuels all of creation. The Hekate presented in the fragments of this mystery poem dating from the second century CE is all powerful. There are several different epithets used to describe Hekate as the World Soul, including Soteira, the Savior. This isn't passive salvation being discussed but refers to the ability of an individual's soul to ascend to higher consciousness through specific acts, including living a magical life.

The Hekate within Us

To explain how we make magic, we need to talk about how Hekate as the World Soul is represented in each of us within our individual souls. In my thinking, each one of us has a soul that is a unique transcendent spirit. This soul is never born into human form but is attached to each incarnation. The soul is connected to our current existence, but we can be disconnected from it for a variety of reasons. I believe that our life's work is to become unified with our soul. By listening to the soul, we can achieve our true life's purpose. When we quiet ourselves through things like meditation, prayer and ritual, we can become better attuned to our soul-voice within. To make powerful magic, we need to tap into our soul-fire and, through this we connect to the natural energies – that we see as Hekate's three streams – in all things. When we evoke Hekate, we connect directly to her. As such, magic is born from the union of the trio of our soul, the soul-fire in all things and Hekate herself.

The Magic of the World Soul

When we connect to Hekate it is always through the World Soul energy. Each of Her many epithets represents a type of energy contained in the World Soul. We establish communication by reaching into our soul and touching that spark. The mechanism by which we reach into our soul is fueled by the World Soul energy that infuses our every cell. To help you get a better understanding of this rather complex idea, I've included the World Soul Sunrise Ritual. I developed this ritual as part of a devotional project carried out by the members of The Covenant of Hekate.

Exercise: World Soul Journey

I love how the symbolism of the rising sun can be used to help me both understand and connect with Hekate as the World Soul. The rising sun epitomizes Hekate as the World Soul, with the blazing colors sending forth Her energy through all of creation. Honoring Hekate as the World Soul during sunrise allows me to truly feel Her awesome force. If you can't get to an actual sunrise outdoors, feel free to use an image of the sunrise or even hold one in your mind's eye. This is a journey exploring the energy of the World Soul and your own.

Timing and Preparations

The ritual should be held at sunrise if possible. You can consult tables for the exact time in your location. The only thing needed for this ritual is you and the sunrise. I'm using Hekate's Wheel as my visualization model with Hekate as the World Soul being symbolized by the rising sun.

World Soul Sunrise Ritual Procedure

Start just as the sun crests the horizon. Position yourself so you are facing the sunrise. Take several deep relaxing breaths. Clear your mind of the business of everyday thoughts.

Sending Your Energy to Your Surroundings

In your mind's eye see the whole of creation as Hekate's Wheel. Begin by seeing yourself as the six-rayed shape at its center. Turn your attention inward. In this quiet space, your soul comes forward becoming the very essence of your being. Feel the World Soul spark within your own soul reach out to fill your whole body. With several deep, relaxing breaths let the soul energy that now fills you pour into the ground beneath your feet. Then raise both arms above your head. Take several more deep breaths releasing your energy up and out through the top of your head. Next, bring your arms to your heart center and visualize the energy from below and above mingling and then spreading out from your heart. You remain sovereign but are connected to your surroundings.

Extending Your Energy

Once you feel connected to the energy all around you, envision it going further out to all of creation (using the three-coiled snake imagery from Hekate's Wheel if you like) and then to the outer circle that is Hekate as the World Soul. See the emerging sun as the symbol of Hekate as the World Soul. As the sun rises, feel the energy of the World Soul wash over you. Keep your breathing steady. Pause here as you feel that connection. This is Hekate beyond any epithet or words, just pure energy.

Connecting with Hekate, the World Soul

Now visualize the energy pouring from Hekate into you while your energy pours into Her using the sun as the focal point. Spend a few moments doing this, with your breath steady. Feel the unity between your soul and the World Soul.

Disconnecting from the World Soul

As you bask in the glow of the rising sun, let the energy of Hekate fill your being, recharging your own soul spark. When you are ready, slowly begin to disconnect from this energy by pulling away gently. Work your way back down through the serpent of creation and your surroundings until your energy is contained within you once more. Your soul is replenished.

Paying Tribute to Hekate, the World Soul

After you've completed the energetic part of this ritual, pay tribute to Hekate using the chant below. "Anima Mundi" means World Soul in Latin.

Anima Mundi Chant

Hail Hekate, Anima Mundi.
Hail Hekate, Anima Mundi.
Hail Hekate, Anima Mundi.
She who is the very soul of the world,
Within me lives the same spark,
That fuels all of creation,
And birthed the universe.
Hail Hekate, Anima Mundi.
Hail Hekate, Anima Mundi.
Hail Hekate, Anima Mundi.

Goddess of the Under World

While Hekate as the World Soul is very much connected to the sun and the moon, Her dark side as an Under World Goddess is very much aligned with lunar energy. In this role, she is deeply tied to her role as Queen of Witchcraft and all things that go bump in the night. The moon is a symbol of Hekate's light shining through the darkness. Both the moon and Hekate have long been protectors against the night's terrors. This version of the Under World is not the same at all as our modern thinking about hell. This is the Under World of the ancient Greeks. It's where all souls (more or less) ended up. Still, not necessarily a place that people wanted to go to, though. While Hekate is cited as being associated with the Under World in several different ancient texts, it is *The Homeric Hymn to Demeter*[20] that gives us the archetypal view of Hekate. In this tale, Hekate guides Persephone both to and from the Under World. It is only Hekate that comes to poor Persephone's aid when she is despondent over her forced exile to Hades. It is also from this story that the iconic image of Hekate as the guardian lighting our way through life comes. There are many images of Hekate holding torches or lamps on ancient coins, statues and other pieces of artwork. The World Soul and Under World Goddess roles aren't contradictory. Instead they reveal to us that Hekate serves as a guide in all the realms. In the Middle World realm of everyday life, She acts as our Guide, while she is the Gatekeeper to the mysteries of the Upper World and our Guardian during our time in the Under World.

The Three Formed Goddess

Hekate's historical depiction as a three-formed goddess provides us with a method for organizing our understanding of Her as our Guide, Guardian and Gatekeeper. Her three forms have been represented in various ways, including figures of Her with three heads but one body and three complete bodies joined together. In this way, She is seen as representing the three visible phases of the moon – waxing, full and waning and the hidden area where the three forms meet symbolizing the Dark Moon. In historical texts She was also portrayed as part of a trio of Goddesses, including Demeter and Persephone. Her three sides also gave her the ability to see in all directions, rendering Her omnipresent. In contemporary times She has been inserted into the Mother, Maiden, Crone version of the triple goddess in the position of the latter. Our views of the gods, including Hekate, change over time as this modern understanding illustrates.

Hekate's Three Sides

Hekate's three overarching roles as Guardian, Guide and Gatekeeper merge Her portrayal in many ancient texts. From the ancient connection with the moon to the modern neo-pagan version of the triple goddess, the common thread is Hekate in the roles of Guardian, Guide and Gatekeeper. This reflects Hekate's long history as a Three-Formed Goddess but adapts the ancient epithets to our modern understanding. The ancient epithets associated with this model of Hekate are *Enodia, Lampadios and Kleidoukhos*. *Enodia* literally means "of the way" or "at the crossroads" and is most indicative of Her role as a guide for our earth-bound journey. *Lampadios* means "Lamp-bearer," representing Hekate as the light in the darkness of the Under World. Hekate as the Keeper of the Keys sits at the gate of the Upper World, protecting Her mysteries and waiting for us to reach out for each new key along our life's journey. The neo-pagan Triple Goddess model can also be included in this framework, with the maiden guardian of the Under World role of ancient virginal warriors (think about the Amazons), the maternal figure being our guide through life and the Matron rather than Crone being the wise gatekeeper of the heavens.

Gatekeeper

Of course, I am beginning with Hekate as the universal key holder who stands at the gates of her mysteries and our lives, holding forth the keys. This epithet comes from the *Orphic Hymn to Hekate*. This ancient reference has resonated with contemporary devotees and the key has become one of the major symbols associated with Hekate today. Hekate holds the keys to the mysteries of the universe and for unlocking the doors in our lives. Hekate as the Gatekeeper is associated with our Higher Selves and Integrity. In this role She also holds the keys to death and life. As such, She is associated with Death and ascension to the heavenly realm. In this role She is seen as Matron, the wise older woman governing the intellect. You can use the term "Crone" if you prefer, but I've long seen Hekate as the Matron so I've used this term instead.

Guide

The meaning of Hekate as Guide is two-fold. The modern application of Hekate as *Enodia* is that Hekate is both the road representing our journey through this life and our guide along the way. I think that we are all born with a predestined road map that we should follow through any one incarnation. However, there are things that happen that cause us to veer off track. That's when her role as Guide along our Middle World journey becomes so important. She'll be there to help us get back on the right path. The energy of Hekate as Guide is that of actions and is associated with kindness. When we think about the true nature of kindness, it is doing what is in another person's best interest (or our own). This sometimes requires not being nice. This is maternal Hekate, the mother figure who supports us, but who also keeps us in line.

Guardian

This leads us to Hekate as the light-bearer, guarding us against the terrors of the darkness. When we are in the lonely cave or deep in a personal Under World, She is there shining her torches of protection over our emotions. Her guardianship extends to our Lower Self where we can struggle with our shadow side. She also guards our passion, helping us to use our intensity for the highest good. Her image as the lamp-bearing guardian is explored throughout this course.

Exercise: Establishing a Daily Meditative Practice

In meditation, we practice controlling our naturally busy minds and focusing our attention. There are many different types of meditations. I use a lot of guided meditations including spiritual journeys in this course and in my personal practice. These meditations use the power of imagery to connect us with the metaphysical realms, receive messages and expand our understanding of the mysteries. Other types of guided meditations focus on unifying our energies, either internally or with external forces. Then there are meditation techniques that seek to clear the mind entirely so there is no use of imagery. Chants, also called mantras, are often used in these types of meditations. By focusing our attention on repeating a short series of sounds or words, we can calm our monkey-minds. Chanting is included in the Witch's Hour of Power.

The words we use in a chant are very powerful, so careful consideration needs to be given to the ones we use. The chant creates the energy of the meditation that we will carry with us through the day. Personally, I do the Three Keys chant every morning. I also do different Sanskrit ones to match my current energetic focus. The Three Keys chant will help you strengthen your connection to Hekate as well. It's important to have a basic practice to foster what can be achieved by incorporating the Three Keys Chant into your Witch's Hour of Power.

The Three Keys Chant

The basic chant is:
Hekate, Guardian.
Hekate, Guide.
Hekate, Gatekeeper.

You can do the chant in English or use the Greek:
Hekate, Lampadios.
Hekate, Enodia.

Hekate, Kleidoukhos.

You can add the three principles as affirmations to your chanting:
I am kind.
I am passionate.
I have integrity.

The three characteristics of the witch's mind can also be added as affirmations:
I am curious.
I am observant.
I am inspired.

You can add other epithets of Hekate or your own affirmations or work with the neo-pagan Triple Goddess model of Maiden, Mother, Matron. Working with a series of three phrases works well with energetic breathing. If you're new to chanting as meditation, then I suggest you start with the Three Keys for at least a week and then adjust it to reflect your intentions for the day ahead, whether you do the meditation before bedtime or first thing in the morning. It helps to balance the mind and keep you grounded. When you add personal affirmations, it helps you stay focused on your intention for the day.

Breathing techniques are very helpful in achieving the balanced state that we seek in meditation. Awareness of the power of our breath reminds us that we are energetic beings, fueled by this energy. In the Three Keys chant, we use a controlled breathing practice based on pranayama techniques from yoga. This further focuses our attention and enhances our connection to Hekate's energetic currents. The point of the chant is not to summon Hekate but to gently connect with Her energy currents that imbue all living things.

Preparing for the Chant

You should prepare yourself for the chanting by washing up. The chanting should take place in a quiet environment with your Statement of Dedication and your image of Hekate placed near you. Study your image of Hekate and the Statement of Dedication for a few minutes prior to beginning. Close your eyes during the ritual. If you are already familiar with breath work and chanting, then this may be easy for you. However, if this is a new experience, take your time getting used to it. I recommend a minimum of nine rounds of the chant as a daily practice. You may want to begin with fewer, perhaps and you can certainly do more. The chanting meditation is designed to take only a few minutes each day. Wearing comfortable clothes, you should sit comfortably with nothing crossed. The room should be quiet, with the lights dimmed. Have your journal handy to record any messages that may come forward during the chanting. It's helpful to count the rounds using your finger tips or by holding nine beads or stones in one hand and passing them to the other after each round.

Chanting Procedure

For the first week or so of doing the Three Keys Chant, you should prime yourself by entering a meditative state using the counting techniques outlined previously. Once you get in the habit of doing the Three Keys Chant, you won't need to do the priming first, as your ability to shift consciousness improves. Don't do the part about unifying the Three Selves, just the counting on either end. You can use this technique to prepare for entering an altered state for any purpose. With practice, the necessity of counting yourself in and out of the trance state will diminish, but, for now, do it this way. Once you have entered the meditative state, you can begin the chanting ritual. After you've completed the 9 recitations, don't forget to count your way back to normal consciousness.

For each of the nine rounds, begin by taking in a deep,

relaxing breath. When you breathe out say the first word, then on your in-breath say the second word, then take a full breath in, move on to the next line with your out breath, like this:

Breathe in … saying "Hail" while you breathe out say "Hekate" and then as you breathe in say "The" … out breath "Way" and so on. This takes a bit of practice to do it out loud, but it's worth it. If you can't do it this way yet, concentrate on saying the words in your head in keeping with your breath. Keep practicing.

After three rounds, pause for three breaths. We're doing this in threes as this is the most powerful number associated with Hekate. When you have recited the chant 9 times, finish by thanking Hekate for Her presence. Don't forget to write about any messages that you receive and your experiences during the chanting.

Daily Chanting Practice

The more you do this chanting exercise, the stronger your relationship with Hekate will become and the better you'll be at summoning Her. It has the added bonuses of helping strengthen your ability to enter an altered state and increasing your attention skills.

Summary

Hekate's complex history provides us with a rich resource about her nature, roles and characteristics. From antiquity, Hekate presents Herself as the Mother of All, the World Soul and the torch-bearing guardian of the Under World. As a three-formed goddess, she is viewed as all-knowing and often as part of a trio of Moon Goddesses. In the Keeping Her Keys model, Hekate's three forms are interpreted as Guardian, Guide and Gatekeeper. Using this tripartite framework as a focus in a daily meditation practice helps to strengthen our connection to Hekate and to hone our attention skills.

Lesson 5: Hekate's Characteristics

I often work with specific epithets for various. There may be certain characteristics of Hekate that I want to pull forward for help with spells or to honor through devotional rituals. Since there are over 200 known epithets from the various ancient sources available for us to call upon, there is no shortage of aspects of Hekate that we can work with.

Hekate as Guardian can be described in many ways, but the most powerful image is that of Her wielding her torches to lead us through the darkness. Hekate Chthonia represents Her as an Under World goddess, while as Nykhia she wanders the night hunting down the terrors and protecting us from them. However, She is also our Savior during these dark times. Hekate Enodia, our Middle World Guide, reflects the vitality necessary to support our earth-bound journeys. As Ergatis, She is the energy fueling the road beneath our feet, while as Kyria She lends us the power and strength required to live our personal truth. Hegemonen is one of the epithets that directly describe Her as a guide, reinforcing this part of Her three-formed nature.

As the Gatekeeper, She is the eternal glorious Key Holder who stands before the gate – *Athanatos Kydmios Kleidoukhos Propylaia*. This is Hekate who governs the cycle of death and birth, the Upper World and intellect.

Sources of Epithets

The ancient epithets, and their sources, should not be taken as dogma. Consider that these are modern interpretations of ancient writings. These epithets are interpreted in a contemporary manner. Once you begin to work with them yourself, you'll discover your own personal understandings of Hekate's roles and characteristics. The ancient epithets can seem to be contradictory. Hekate is benevolent in one instance, then She is the Flesh Eater in another. This is because the ancients would ascribe whatever characteristic of a deity was necessary to get the job done, whether a spell, prayer, hymn or story.

The major source of ancient knowledge of Hekate's epithets is The Greek Magical Papyri.[20] The Chaldean Oracles[21] and The Orphic Hymn to Hekate[22] are additional significant sources. Then there are various other hymns, defixiones (curse tablets), fragments, and other objects (such as coins). The Greek Magical Papyri is a collection of ancient rituals, prayers and spells from Graeco-Roman Egypt, between the second century BCE to the fifth century of the common era. There are multiple sources and authors. The characteristics that we work with in this course that come from the *PGM* include *Nykhia* and *Kydmios*. Hekate's role as Guardian comes from this source as well. Many of the spells in the PGM invoke Hekate in one of her Under World aspects, such as *Drakaina* (Of Dragons), *Kardiodaitos* (Eater of Men's Hearts), and Nekyia (Mistress of Corpses). One of my favorites focuses on calling upon Hekate Nekyia, drowning a cat and then summoning its daimon (spirit) to do the caster's dirty work:

> I call upon you, Mother of All ... Mistress of Corpses, Hekate, I conjure you, The daimon aroused ... Go and perform the deed.

The PGM also contains many epithets that reflect Hekate in more kind roles, including multiple names that invoke Her as Mother of All (e.g., Geneteira, Pammetor). Then there are less familiar aspects of Hekate, including *Erototokos* (Producing Love) and *Kalliste* (Fairest).

In contrast, The Chaldean Oracles are a group of fragments from an ancient poem dating to the second century CE. The Hekate presented in these fragments is that of the World Soul, Savior, and even the Fiery Rose of Creation:

... from there, a lightning-bolt, sweeping along, obscures the rose (flower) of fire as it leaps into the hollows of the worlds. For from there, all things begin to extend wonderful rays down below. (Fragment 34)

The Orphic Hymn to Hekate

The Orphic Hymn to Hekate is another important source of epithets, it is the source for two of Hekate's Roles: *Enodia* and *Kleidoukhos*. In addition, we also use the characteristics of *Chthonia* and *Hegemonen* from this source.

Other Ancient Sources

There are many other ancient sources describing Hekate. *Propylaia* comes from a description of Greece,[23] while Kratais is used in the story of Jason and the Argonauts.[24]

Using Hekate's Epithets

Although it is entirely up to you, I recommend starting with Hekate's Triple Goddess roles (Guardian, Guide and Gatekeeper) to evoke Hekate at the beginning of any working, and then move on to specific ones that reflect your intentions using the nine core characteristics. Typically, the ancient Greek version of the epithet is said followed by the modern application. The energy of the epithets can be utilized by reciting them and by representing them in writing.

Reciting the Epithets

When we speak the epithets, their ancient power is released into the world, signalling Hekate that we are seeking her attention. Careful consideration should be given to using the epithets. Take time to familiarize yourself with them before using them in rituals. Although consulting with online Greek language resources can help with pronunciation, I recommend that you say them in the manner that is comfortable for you. The way to say a certain epithet may come naturally to you or you may have to practice for a while.

Representing the Epithets in Writing

Writing the epithets is incredibly powerful and is usually used in conjunction with reciting them. You can create your own set of the Hekate's three roles and the nine characteristics that you can use repeatedly. This can be done on heavy paper, rocks, or pieces of wood.

Epithets Can be Worked with in a Variety of Ways

1. We can choose one or more epithets to be the core aspect of Hekate that we work with
2. We can select epithets for a ritual or spell
3. We can use the cycles of nature to explore the epithets

The epithets that we work with can change over time, or we can stay committed to one core epithet. There's no one correct way to work with the epithets.

Exercise: Feeling the Power of the Epithets

For the week before you do the exercise with the written epithets, you should focus on your own feelings as much as possible. Record the circumstances in which you feel either love energy or fear energy. As you are recording them, take notice of the emotions that accompany this activity. Even after the event has passed, you can call up those emotions by merely writing about them. Contemplate the energetic power of emotions. Go through a few examples in detail so you can understand your own emotions better. A good technique is to intentionally call a memory to mind, write about it, and then observe your own emotional state.

Here are a few examples of the different emotions classified as either love or fear-based:

- Love emotions: kindness, contentment, joy, love, kindness, responsibility.
- Fear emotions: anger (not the compassionate kind), despair, depression, anxiety, loneliness, sadness, rage.

Exploring Love and Fear Using Hekate's Epithets

After you've completed at least a couple of the written explorations of your emotions, it's time to use that skill of emotional identification when it comes to using Hekate's epithets for devotion, personal development or witchcraft. You're going to create love and fear energy using Hekate's epithets. This will be accomplished by selecting the epithets and then doing a chanting exercise to summon the energy associated with either the fear of love-based epithets.

The epithets are listed in alphabetical order. Pick three that feel right to you.

Instructions

From the list below, select three epithets each that reflect love and fear energy (for a total of six). Copy each of set of epithets onto paper or make a representation of them in some other way. Place one set of epithets on your altar. I highly recommend starting with your fear-based epithets in case there is any residual energy left after the first round of chanting. The love-based ones will cancel out lingering effects.

Fear-based epithets: *Atasthalos* (Wicked), *Nykhia* (Night Walker), *Phoberos* (Fearful), *Polyonumos* (Sufferer), *Pyripnoa* (Fire Breather) and *Skotia* (Gloomy). These reflect Under World energy and are represented by the color black.

Love-based epithets: *Aglaos* (Pleasing), *Erotokos* (Bearer of Love), *Kalliste* (Fairest), *Melinoe* (Soothing), *Paionios* (Healer) and *Tletos* (Patient). The energetic realm is the Upper World, symbolized by white.

Prepare sacred space and yourself as you learned in the previous exercises. Ask Hekate to bless and protect your working. Ask her to let you temporarily feel the energy of your chosen fear-based epithets:

Hail Hekate, Guardian,
Hail Hekate, Guide,
Hail Hekate, Gatekeeper.
Protect me,
Guide me
Open the gate of understanding.
May I feel the power of these epithets
To better know myself and You.

Then chant the epithets in that group as a sequence for three minutes. Notice the emotive energy in your sacred space and your own emotional state. When you are finished chanting the fear-based epithets, take them and either burn them or rip them up and throw them in the trash. You'll want to get them out of your home right away. Once you've destroyed them, ask Hekate to release their energy from you:

Hail Hekate, Guardian,
Hail Hekate, Guide,
Hail Hekate, Gatekeeper.
Cleanse this space of all the energy of the fear-based epithets.
Release me from their power.

Now place the other set (the love-based ones) on your altar. Start by evoking Hekate once again using the text above. Chant these three epithets as a sequence for three minutes, repeating the process from the fear-based set. Again, notice the energy in your sacred space and your own emotions.

Thank Hekate for her presence again, then open your sacred space. You may want to keep some of that loving feeling rather than asking Hekate to take it all away:

Hail Hekate, Guardian,
Hail Hekate, Guide,
Hail Hekate, Gatekeeper.
May Your love energy remain with me,
Thank You for Your presence at my working.

After the Exercise

Compare the energy that was created just doing this simple chanting exercise.

This is an example of how powerful emotional energy is in our magic. Journal about your experience.

Using the Epithets to Honor Hekate

We can honor certain aspects of Hekate as a means of expressing gratitude. For example, when we successfully obtain a new key in life, we can give offerings to Hekate as Gatekeeper, the Keeper of the Keys. We can also make offerings to a characteristic of Hekate that we want to pull forward into our lives. An example of this would be if we wanted to transition to a new phase in life, we could make offerings to Hekate as Guide and use the epithet of *Enodia*. Throughout the course, we'll talk about specific ways of using the epithets in this manner and there are exercises for you to do using the epithets. Continuing with this example, we could draw upon this aspect of Our Lady to cast a spell as a means of conjuring the change we seek.

Using the Epithets in Witchcraft

Each epithet is a current emanating from Hekate extending to all of creation. See the energy as a key that Hekate will (at least temporarily) give you access to. It's important to keep in mind that Hekate's energy can't easily be cajoled or manipulated into doing your bidding. The way I use epithets in witchery is by carefully developing my intention and then exploring which epithet best suits the nature of my planned working. I often work with multiple epithets, usually in sets of threes since this is the number most associated with Her. I often start the exaltations of any working with summoning Her as Guardian, Guide and Gatekeeper. Then I select subsequent epithets that are more closely related to my intention from the list of core characteristics. I typically layer in other ideas and my own contemporary interpretations for the epithets within the text of a spell. That way the spell has a great deal of meaning.

Using the Epithets in Personal Development Work

Epithets can also be used to reflect a characteristic of ourselves that we wish to develop using our own skills and Hekatean energy. The epithets aren't to be used in a passive manner, just like any sort of devotion or witchery, saying a few words and then doing nothing will get you nowhere. Always remember that Hekate can't do for us what She can't do through us. Sometimes, we wish to petition Hekate as a specific epithet that we don't want anything to do with personally. For example, if I am hanging onto painful memories, I may offer this up to Hekate as *Chthonia* and ask Her to relieve me of my hurt by taking it straight to the Under World.

Exercise: Starting Your Book of Shadows

A witch's Book of Shadows is their record of their magical and devotional workings. There are countless ways to make your Book of Shadows, so I'm not going to get too much into the details. You may already have an established one. If that's the case, then I recommend continuing with it, unless you feel strongly that you need to start fresh. It can be a regular notebook, a binder or a hand-crafted masterpiece. Pinterest is a great place to look for ideas for designing your Book. I use fancy spiral-bound hard cover notebooks. I prefer these – I've used lots of different types – because they are easy to hold onto during workings. My Book of Shadows is separate from my personal journal. I highly recommend that you do the same because the energy of our personal journals can be quite intense, especially if we are doing deep healing work. A degree of separation between our innermost thoughts and our Book of Shadows is a good idea to avoid mixing up energies. The journal is your place to let it all out, while the Book of Shadows is a more organized and structured account of your magical workings. Speaking of organization, I use the pages with the pockets on them for keeping important reference materials in. I make cards of the lunar phases, important dates, Hekate's Wheel of the Year, etc.

My Book of Shadows extends to my laptop where I have documents, e-books, lists of things and the many databases that I create. I've got spreadsheets for Hekate's epithets, Her garden and lots more. A witch's Book of Shadows can be whatever you want it to be. Typical contents of a Book of Shadows includes information about Hekate and her epithets, prayers, meditations, rituals, sacred space, correspondences, herbs, divination work, and spells.

On the first page of your Book of Shadows you can make a cover page with designs, symbols and other magical images. You can draw them or use existing pictures. Be creative. As you construct your title page, concentrate on the intention for your Book. When the title page is finished, I recommend doing a dedication ritual. It's doesn't have to be elaborate. You can ask Hekate to bless the contents and the magic you'll make with the Book. Add a statement of commitment for using the book for the highest good and end with, "My intention is true and my will is strong."

Practice: Learning the Orphic Hymn to Hekate

The first entry in the Book of Shadows should be one of dedication to Hekate. I'm recommending The *Orphic Hymn to Hekate* (1st–3rd CE). I often recite it during devotional work. I've copied it in my Book of Shadows, made social media posts using it, and, perhaps most importantly, I've turned to it repeatedly as a source of inspiration when writing my own workings. It's a most fitting first entry. Say the Orphic Hymn as often as you like. Reciting it will help you learn the various characteristics of Our Lady Hekate and will strengthen your connection to Her. You can embellish the Hymn with Hekate's symbols and whatever else feels right. There is debate about whether it's appropriate to share your Book. I personally don't let anyone see the book, although I share from it by copying things into a different format.

The Orphic Hymn to Hekate

I invoke you, beloved Hekate of the Crossroads and the Three Ways

Saffron-cloaked Goddess of the Heavens, the Underworld and the Sea

Tomb-frequenter mystery-raving with the souls of the dead

Daughter of Perses, Lover of the Wilderness who walks amongst the deer

Night going One, Protectress of dogs,

Unconquerable Queen

Beast-roarer, Dishevelled One of compelling countenance

Tauropolos, Keyholding Mistress of the universe

Ruler, Nymph, Mountain-wandering Nurturer of the young

Maiden, I beg you to be present at these sacred rites

Forever with a happy heart and gracious to the cattle.

Other Roles of Hekate

While the *Orphic Hymn* contains many of Hekate's characteristics and aspects, She is much more than what is portrayed in it. Two other aspect of Our Lady that are particularly relevant to the practice of Modern Hekatean Witchcraft are Goddess of Witchcraft and Guardian of the Marginalized.

Hekate, Goddess of Witchcraft

Associated with Hekate's Under World aspects is her role as the Goddess of Witchcraft. The origins of this title are tricky to pinpoint, but the earliest known references come from antiquity. In the stories about Medea, we see her call out to Hekate to help with her spells.[25] She was certainly viewed by some in the ancient world as the Goddess of Witchcraft, Darkness, and Ghosts. There is evidence of what could be labelled witch cults devoted to Hekate during antiquity, and She was definitely associated with magic in the ancient world.[26] During Roman times, Hekate was often seen as part of a triad of moon goddesses.[27] However, our modern understanding is heavily influenced by the Diana/Hecate (Latin spelling) cults that grew during the eighteenth–twentieth centuries.[28] However, recent books on Hekate, such as *Circle for Hekate: Volume 1,* have helped us to see that Hekate as a Goddess of Witchcraft is not limited to Her Under World aspects.[29]

Guardian of the Marginalized

Connected to the shift in perception of Hekate away from a narrow view of her as an Under World deity towards a broader understanding has been the contemporary interpretation of Hekate as a guardian of the marginalized.[30] This application is an important consideration because of the principles of kindness and integrity. The ancient evidence that is used to apply this modern title to Hekate comes from several sources. First and foremost, in her capacity as the World Soul, Hekate is the very essence of all of creation. In addition, Hekate *Pammetor,* or the Mother of All, highlights Her maternal role for all humans, including the most vulnerable.

Her roles as *Kourotrophos,* Guardian of Children, and *Eileithyia*, Nurse of Childbirth, highlight Her special consideration to children and women, both often vulnerable groups in ancient times and today. Beyond these epithets, and her connection to witches, there are no specific associations of Her with marginalized groups. However, there are many other representations that associate Her with the vulnerable, notably her roles as Helper (*Aregos*), Healer (*Paionos*), and Savior (*Soteira*). She is also referred to as all nurturing (*Pantrophos*), tender (*Atala*) and an evil destroyer (*Alexeatis*), all very useful traits when working to reduce inequalities. Moreover, Her various epithets associated with strength (e.g., *Adamantaea, Alkimos, Kratais*) and transformation (e.g., *Ameibousa, Dadouchos, Phosphoros*) all provide beneficial energy to the vulnerable. For me, these epithets combined lend considerable evidence that Hekate is Guardian of the Marginalized.

Understanding Hekate

I hope these last two lessons have made you curious to learn more about Hekate, both in the intellectual sense and in terms of truly understanding her. Researching Hekate, whether through direct study of the modern interpretations of the ancient texts or by reading others' thoughts on these writings is a very worthwhile undertaking. I think that Hekate desires us to be well-informed critical thinkers rather than blind adherents to anyone else's version of her. To me, there is a big difference between knowing about Hekate and knowing her.

When we know Hekate, we begin to understand her mighty powers and become more skilled at invoking her presence for our witchcraft. In time, we can learn to tap into her energy currents as well. Truly knowing Hekate requires understanding beyond anything that can be found through the works of others or our attempts to reproduce rituals – we must experience her.

Experiencing Hekate

There are many ways to experience Hekate. Since she is such a diverse all-purpose goddess, we may be drawn to one aspect of hers (or a handful) or we may feel connected to Hekate in her totality. We may have an initial experience with Hekate where she presents herself in a complete vision that is entirely experiential, or we may experience her after we have already read a lot. The more we experience Hekate, the more we understand her. This understanding enables us to become better at witchcraft as we develop the skills necessary to involve her and her energies in our workings.

Summary

Hekate's characteristics are described in the many epithets assigned to Her. An epithet is the term that describes a feature of a deity. We work with these epithets by evoking the specific energies that are connected to them either by reciting them or representing them in writing. Your Book of Shadows is your record of all your workings using Hekate's Modern Witchcraft, including your notes about Her roles and epithets. It's also the place to record ancient hymns, prayers and other texts. The first entry in your Book of Shadows should be very special, such as *The Orphic Hymn to Hekate*. The epithets can be classified as reflecting either fear or love energy. Being able to connect to these energies at will is an important skill for witches to develop. Learning about Hekate's three roles and epithets is important to practicing Her modern witchcraft, but the most important thing is to understand Hekate as She presents Herself to us. This can only be achieved through direct experience.

Lesson 6: Honoring Hekate

We honor Hekate best through our personal development work. As such, devotion is a very active process that serves to strengthen our relationship with Hekate. In this lesson, we'll explore the various offerings and rituals that we make to express our gratitude to Hekate and to seek Her blessings. The main focal point of the monthly calendar is the astrological New Moon when two rituals are performed. The first is one of gratitude to Hekate and the second is our personal commitment for the upcoming month in terms of our personal development. We'll get to that later, but first let's discuss the role of offerings.

Offerings

An offering is a symbolic gesture to Hekate demonstrating our affection and gratitude. The offerings we make to Hekate should be appropriate both in the historical sense and for your personal relationship with Hekate. These gifts are reflections of your devotion, so they should mean a lot to you. In ancient times, animal sacrifices were a common way to seek the favor of a deity. Hekate was no exception – dogs and other animals were often sacrificed to her. While our modern sensibilities don't look positively at this practice, we can harness the energy of animals in expressing devotion in other ways. We can volunteer time at an animal shelter as a form of devotional service, for example.

The traditional offerings from the ancient sources that are suitable for any devotional ritual include edibles and libations. Cakes, fruit and drinks are suitable for a Hekate's Supper. The ancient "cakes" were quite dissimilar from our ideas about these concoctions. Their cakes were more like a mixture of a cheesecake and a scone or a biscuit, but any sort is appropriate. For libations, wine, mead or even beer can be used. If you don't consume alcohol, a sweet beverage can be substituted. Fruit that grew naturally in the Mediterranean region was part of the historical Hekate's Suppers. Examples include pomegranates, plums and dates. There is also an indication that nuts were included, particularly almonds. Alternatively, household scraps were offered consisting of unwanted leftovers. It's important to consider that these ancient offerings were comprised of things that were available and made sense to devotees during those days.

While using the ingredients common in ancient Hekate's Suppers is a fantastic way to honor Our Lady, you shouldn't feel that this is necessary. It's possible to adopt the intent of these ancient suppers by offering food that is meaningful to you and locally sourced. For example, I often use blueberries as an offering. They grow abundantly here in Nova Scotia, I love them, and the local wildlife can safely consume them. That last point is an important one: if you are leaving your offerings outside, ensure that you're not leaving anything noxious to the critters in the area.

We can honor Hekate as the Triple Goddess and the World Soul, or we can worship one of Her many characteristics. I usually work with the triple aspect because I focus on Hekate as Guardian, Guide and the Key. Don't feel this is necessary, though. Do what you feel led to do. Your understanding of Hekate will grow and change over time and your offerings will be reflections of this.

Types of Offerings

Offerings can also be objects that are known to be associated with Hekate, such as plants and objects. Plant offerings suitable include roses, oak leaves and others from Hekate's Garden. There are many plants associated with Hekate. In the lesson entitled Hekate's Garden, we'll be discussing plants in general and the Three Key Herbs of bay laurel, mugwort and sage.

Tokens of appreciation, including keys, crystals or even bones make excellent offerings. We can use a key as an offering when we associate the key with a specific event. For example, I have offered Hekate keys as expressions of gratitude for blessings in my life. I put the key with an edible offering and leave it outside. Bones as symbols of Hekate as Guardian represent the traditional view of the Under World as the home of the dead. This shouldn't be confused with the idea of the Christian definition of hell. Seashells are a type of bone and are highly suitable both as offerings and as containers for placing offerings on. Including bits of ourselves can also be appropriate offerings. I usually limit this to hair clippings but there is a long history of making blood offerings to Hekate. Another offering that I often give Hekate are household sweepings. This may sound weird, but it's based on a historical practice. After you clean your house, either burn or toss outside the sweepings. You can say something like, "Mighty Hekate, I return these sweepings to you so that they can be reborn." If I am not burning the waste, I limit it to scraps that will be eaten by local animals.

Doing activities in service to Hekate is one type of energetic offering. I've already written about my devotional walks and volunteering at an animal shelter. In Her role as Guardian of the Marginalized, we can express our devotion by donating to a suitable charity on or by volunteering our time. Even taking dinner to a homebound person or giving to a panhandler can be acts of devotion. Another energetic offering can be something personal that we wish to give up. Hekate is the Mistress of Rebirth, so she willingly accepts the things that no longer serve us – including painful experiences or self-harmful ways of behaving and thinking. She'll not only gladly accept these re-gifts but will return them to the earth from where they will be reborn.

Sacrifices – not the animal kind – are another form of energetic offering. When we give up something that is important to use, we show our devotion. This can be a two-fold activity where the things we deny ourselves also help with our personal development. This is different than giving Her something that we want to get rid of, it's about giving up something that we need to be free from. Examples can include toxic relationships, addictions and other things that we desire but aren't in our own best interests. The last type of energetic offering that I'm going to discuss are rituals. I encourage you to get creative with your offerings. Researching the historical objects associated with Hekate – beyond what I've included in this course – is a form of devotion in and of itself.

Devotional Rituals

There are many different types of rituals that we do, including magical ones that are part of a spell and devotional ones that are energetic offerings to Hekate. The former will be discussed in the lesson on spell crafting, for now let's discuss the latter. A devotional ritual usually consists of both words and actions that: 1.) seek to establish a connection between ourselves and Hekate and 2.) express gratitude. This is different from when we petition Hekate for guidance and assistance, although the two can be interwoven into one working.

Getting Hekate's Attention

We've discussed how to connect with her in a previous lesson. Those techniques were quite informal. Think of those as sending Her a text message. You'll get a reply, but it's no substitute for a face-to-face encounter or even a chat on the phone. You can see our daily chanting as the line that maintains the connection between us and Hekate – we don't always actively seek Her attention, but we want to have that cord between us. When we use more formal methods of contacting Hekate we are using that cord that we have built and strengthened through our daily chanting practice. Each time we enter this meditative state, we reinforce this cord so that when we wish to get Her attention, we are much more likely to be successful. During a ritual, we typically use formal techniques for calling upon Hekate.

Petitioning Hekate

A petition is a statement seeking the attention and favor of a deity. Through petitioning Hekate, we want her energy to manifest in our presence. This is known as evocation. In contrast, when we invoke a deity or a spirit, we are giving them permission to transgress our sovereignty, so they can take up residence within our mind and body. This is a very different experience from when we receive internal messages from Hekate that we perceive as visions or inner awareness. When Hekate has been invoked into a person, the individual loses their perception of reality. It is a form of possession. I've only invoked Hekate a handful of times during group rituals. I caution against doing this alone, and especially not if you are new to Hekatean energy. The experience of invocation is transformative, but without the proper supports during and after there are risks to your psychological and spiritual well-being. Take this as a caution to focus on evocation rather than invoking Our Lady until you are 100% confident that you can handle the experience.

Evoking Hekate through petitioning is also a very powerful experience. I compare it to the feeling of Her presence that some of us experience either spontaneously or when we are seeking her attention – but only exponentially amplified. When we petition to evoke Hekate, we want Her full presence, not the glimmer characteristic of more informal encounters. Oftentimes, like in the petition below, we use both words and actions to petition for Hekate's presence. I rarely use a full evocation technique. After all, I don't want to summon more of her presence than I need for any working. If I am doing a spell, I may use the evocation or petition Her in a specific role or in conjunction with the energy of one or more correspondence. The following evocation is suitable for any rite. It can be used when you are seeking to honor Our

Lady or at the beginning of a spell.

Exercise: Evoking Hekate

Evocation consists of a powerful petition designed to get the full attention of Hekate. A properly constructed evocation leads to the presence of Our Lady and access to her energy currents. As such, the experience is very intense. This technique is not something to do every day. It's also not something to do in a cavalier manner. Both are types of abusing our ability to petition Hekate and will damage our cord with Her. We may even manage to get on her bad side, which is not someplace anyone wants to be. Use this evocation as appropriate, especially when you genuinely want to honor Hekate.

There are two ways to use this evocation. The first is as is – when you want Hekate's full attention and have no other purpose besides this. The second – the more common use – is when you seek her presence so that you can do something else. The first time you'll do this evocation is to honor Hekate at the Dark Moon, which is discussed in the section immediately after the evocation technique training module. For now, you should determine the date of the Dark Moon, so you can schedule your practice session in such a way that you'll be ready to do the full evocation during the next Dark Moon.

Practicing

I recommend that you begin to practice the evocation technique now. Read it over a few times, practice the hand movements, make notes and contemplate the various parts of it. Say a few words of prayer to Hekate to let Her know that this is what you are doing. Once you are comfortable with the text and actions, work up to doing the full ritual by practicing it one section at a time. Since the goal is to use the evocation at the next Dark Moon, schedule your practice sessions accordingly. You should practice each section at least once before your Dark Moon ritual honoring

Hekate. When you practice, make sure you say a few words to Hekate to let Her know what you are doing and set the intention that the energy of the evocation is only used for the highest good. Begin your practice sessions by saying, "My intention is true, my will is strong and this space is sacred to Hekate only." This will prevent unwanted entities from being attracted to the energy you summon. Even though you're only practicing, Hekate's energy is so powerful that you'll undoubtedly harness Her currents that run through all living things. Practice helps us get comfortable with the force of these streams of energy before we petition Hekate for her full presence.

Book of Shadows Entry

Copy the evocation in your Book of Shadows. Words, both spoken and written, have a lot of power. By recording the evocation in your Book of Shadows, you will add power to the words when you speak them, and it will help you remember them. Read the evocation out of your Book of Shadows.

Preparation

Even when practicing, it's vital that you cleanse yourself. Wash your hands, remove your make-up, change your clothes and make sure the space is tidy. I recommend you engage in standard ritual preparation before you start any working, including proper cleansing and consecration of all objects and tools to be used and a self-purification including bathing. You'll need to place a new candle on your altar when you do the full evocation ritual. During practice, you can start with a new candle, but relight it during each session. Don't use this same candle for the full evocation because it will be full of your energy from your trial runs. There's nothing else that you need for this ritual, except the most important things – confidence and focus. One thing I know for certain is that Hekate will not attend my rites if I am not completely *into it*. Lacking confidence, being distracted or not having faith in Her and my abilities are all impediments to Her favor.

Timing
Practice sessions can be done anytime. The ritual itself should be done on the time best suited for your specific working.

Location
You should practice in front of your altar and do the full evocation in the same location until you feel comfortable with the energetic focal point of the altar boosting your cord to Hekate.

Creating the Energetic Circle
Stand directly in front of it and take three steps back. From this perspective, focus all your attention on your image of Hekate. Envision a protective circle around you and the altar. With your right hand extended make three large clock-wise circles, creating a sphere of contained energy all around you. This space can only be permeated by Hekate, either as the energy currents or the life force in all things with Her presence. Say "my intention is true, my will is strong and this space is sacred to Hekate only" repeatedly as you cast the circle.

Hand Positions
There are hand positions that go with the evocation. The basic way to hold your hands is together, with the three middle fingers of each hand touching each other; this is known as the *kleis* (Greek for key) position. This symbol represents interconnections among the three aspects of Hekate, our three selves and the three worlds in our extended but touching fingers. The unity of these is expressed through the circle we make with our thumb and little finger. The position itself is based on the Buddhi Mudra in Yoga. Your thumb and pinky finger of the same hand should be together, forming a circle. Start with your hands in the Middle

World position, at your heart center. Although your hands don't always remain touching, each hand stays in the same position – with the three fingers out and the thumb-pinky in a circle. The left hand always moves down to the earth, while the right will reach up each time.

Evocation of Hekate Suitable for Any Rite Text

Part 1 – Evocation of Hekate's Three Forms
(Hands together at heart center)
Blessed Hekate, Great Mother, I am grateful for Your presence
 in my life.
I implore You, attend this rite.
Great Hekate, who spins the web of the stars and governs the
 spiral of life.
I welcome you as Guardian, Queen of the Under World,
 I welcome you as Guide of the Middle World,
 I welcome you as Gatekeeper of the Mysteries.

Part 2: Evocation of the Energy Currents
Fierce Goddess, Attend your epithets!
I draw upon Your colors!
(Left hand down)
 Black as night,
(Hands together at heart center)
Red as blood,
(Right hand to the sky)
White as stars.
 (Hands together at heart center)
Lend me their energies,
 I implore you, Mighty Queen!
I offer myself to You.
I bow before You,
Hear me, know my name.

(Bow your head, state your name.)

Part 3: Evocation of the Three Forms
(Left hand down) Hail Hekate
(Right hand up) Hail Hekate
(Hands together at heart center) Hail Hekate
I honor You as She of all forms.
(Left hand down)
    I honor You as the Young Mistress,
And ask that You bestow upon this ritual the energy of youth.
(Hands at heart center)
    I honor You as the Eternal Creatrix,
And ask that You send the power of creation to my working.
(Right hand up)
    I honor You as the timeless World Soul,
And ask that You lend me your wisdom for this rite.

Part 4: Evocation of the Three Realms
(Left hand down) Hail Hekate
(Right hand up) Hail Hekate
(Hands together at heart center) Hail Hekate
I honor you as She who rules over
    The Under World, the Middle World and the Upper World.
(Left hand down)
I honor You as the Gatekeeper of All Under World and Goddess
    of the Daemon
May they strengthen my rite!
(Hands together at heart center)
I honor You as the Guardian of the Crossroads of the Middle
    World, the Universal Key Holder,
And seek Your guidance along my earth-bound journey.
(Right hand up)
I honor You as the Breath of the Universe and the Mother of
    Angels

Behold, I seek their assistance now!
(Left hand down) Hail Hekate
(Right hand up) Hail Hekate
(Hands together at heart center) Hail Hekate

Part 5: Evocation of the Three Dominions
I honor You as Sovereign over land, sea and sky.
(Left hand down)
I honor You as Queen of the Sea
And petition for Your mighty waves to strengthen my desire.
(Hands together at heart center)
I honor You as Queen of the Land
And ask that You hasten my working on the earthly plane.
(Right hand up)
I honor You as Queen of the Sky
And implore your assistance across the higher realm.
(Left hand down) Hail Hekate
(Right hand up) Hail Hekate
(Hands together at heart center) Hail Hekate

Part 5: Evocation of the Three Keys
(Left hand down)
I honor You as Guardian, Eternal Torch Bearer,
And ask that Your light shine on this working.
(Right hand up)
I honor You as the Gatekeeper,
And pray that You'll open the doors to your mysteries.
(Hands to heart center)
I honor You as the Guide along my path,
And petition your favor.

Part 6: Evocation of Queen of Witches
(Hands together at heart center)
I honor You as Queen of the Witches,

And ask Your blessing for this rite!
My intention is pure
And my will is strong!

Ending the evocation

If you are only doing the evocation without any additional focus (i.e., a spell), you'll end the evocation by opening the energetic circle that you created at the beginning of the ritual. Do to this, extend your left arm straight in front of you, parallel to the floor. Focus your attention on your extended index finger of your left hand. Envision all the energy you've summoned coming together at the tip of this finger. While Hekate cannot be contained, She will comprehend what you are doing and immediately start to retreat. Once you have achieved this focus, say "Hail Mighty Hekate, thankful am I for your presence at this ritual, I bid you farewell." Now open the space by reversing the circle by making three large ones with your finger in a counter clockwise direction. You'll be able to feel the shift in the space as you open it. After the circle is open, take some time to return to your body, using the meditation technique of counting that was described in an earlier lesson.

The Lunar Cycle

As you practice the evocation leading up to the Dark Moon ritual honoring Hekate, it's a good time to contemplate the role of the moon in Modern Hekatean Witchcraft. Like time, the moon is always changing. This ever-different energy provides us with the ultimate correspondence available for us to use in our workings. The lunar cycle consists of five distinct phases. On the first day of the month, the Dark Moon, Hekate is honored through devotional acts on the Deipnon. The second day of the cycle is Noumenia, the time for acknowledging Hekate as matron of our personal lives and homes, and for doing workings to set our intentions for the new cycle. As the moon waxes towards its fullness, is the time for doing magic that focuses on attraction energy. The Full Moon is an optimal time for all type of spellwork. Then as the moon wanes back towards the Deipnon, our focus is on reversal and removal magic.

The Full Moon is not specifically a day for honoring Hekate, although many practitioners do. For me, the Full Moon is a time to work magic on whatever I am trying to conjure up. The waning moon is a time to subtract things using magic, while the waxing moon should be used for adding things. Just about any intention can be crafted into a spell at any time of the month. During the waning moon, it is especially appropriate to offer Hekate gifts that are dead or decaying, while during the waxing moon, offerings should be livelier (e.g., recently cut roses).

The Deipnon

The importance of the Deipnon (Dark Moon) in Modern Hekatean Witchcraft can't be overstated. This is the beginning of the new cycle, the astrological New Moon. The power of the moon on this day is equal to that of the Full Moon. Each lunar cycle, devotees make offerings, write prayers, do rituals, and engage in activities (for example, community service) that honor Hekate. Our contemporary Deipnon is based on the ancient practice of holding a Hekate's Supper on the first evening of the new lunar cycle. The ancient Greeks viewed the day as starting at sundown, so after this on the first day of the cycle a meal would be left for Hekate at a three-way crossroads.

Honoring Hekate on the Dark Moon

This is a time for expressing devotion to Hekate. The word "devotion" may seem odd to you, I know it did when I first heard it applied to a deity. Devotion means being committed to Hekate. Even that sounds a tad strange. What it means is that you have a relationship with her wherein you are committed to honoring her through various activities. Devotion to Hekate requires the same attitude being applied to ourselves. We honor both ourselves and Hekate by living a magical life, practicing witchcraft and expressing our devotion. The Deipnon is the time we set aside as a special day for honoring Hekate. This can be celebrated in diverse ways. You can adapt the traditional Hekate's Supper, you can create a personal ritual based on your understanding of Hekate or any other activity that makes sense to you. Any of the offerings previously discussed are appropriate. I typically go on what I call a devotional walk to the place where I perform my Deipnon ritual. During this walk, I'll do various versions of the Three Keys chant, recite a list of epithets and some excerpts from the ancient texts. I also often do the Evocation of Hekate that you've been practicing.

Exercise: Dark Moon Ritual

In general, it's best to start work on the Deipnon Ritual the day after the Full Moon. This way you'll have lots of time to contemplate what your intention is, to plan your offerings, and write your devotional hymn.

- What is your intention: Do you want to focus on specific blessings you've received? Will you be using certain epithets?
- Choose the offerings that best match your intention.
  - If you are working with particular epithets, select offerings that correspond to them. For example, you may be honoring Hekate as Gatekeeper, so offerings of keys would make sense.
- Design your altar for the ritual. What correspondences, objects and tools will you be using?
- Select music if you'll be using it.
- Choosing the ritual:
  - Doing an existing one – such as using the Evocation of Hekate Suitable for Any Rite or using the Orphic

Hymn.

o Writing your own ritual script:

- A ritual script can be called many things – a hymn, a prayer or petition are examples. A hymn is generally just a piece of poetry, prose or song that is about Hekate and a prayer or petition are to Her.

- Start with the opening welcome to Hekate, including any epithets that you are honoring. This summoning of Hekate is known as the exaltation.

- State your intention as it corresponds to the epithets being called upon.

- Offer your gratitude for Her protection and blessings and bid her farewell at the end.

- Set up your offerings beside your image of Hekate. Light a candle and then recite your hymn, prayer or do the evocation.

Understanding: Processing Your Deipnon Ritual

After the ritual, you should write about the experience in your journal, recording how you felt, how you perceived Hekate and any messages you may have received from Her while doing it. If things don't go perfectly, make sure you write about the specifics of what went wrong. I find that's how I've learned the most about witchcraft – through my mistakes.

Practice: Developing a Gratitude Attitude

When we engage in intentional gratitude, we acknowledge the abundance present in our lives. This opens the cord of prosperity, drawing even more good things to us. I'm not talking about hokey law of attraction energy; I'm talking about witch power. We create the energy, we do the work and we get things done. Developing a gratitude attitude is a sure-fire way to increase our personal prosperity and to augment any magic we may have going on. A regular gratitude practice is part of the Witches'

Hour of Power. If you don't already practice daily intentional gratitude, now is the time to begin. It's so simple. First thing in the morning before you even get out of bed, express your gratitude for one thing. It can be anything, from a goodnight's sleep to the day ahead or for Hekate's presence in your life. Practice this technique for a week and I guarantee you'll see a difference in all areas of your life.

Noumenia

The day after the Deipnon is known as Noumenia. This is the day to set our intentions for the new lunar cycle and to seek Hekate's blessing over it. In addition, we can use the traditional theme of the day by petitioning Hekate to watch over our home. There is some debate as to whether it is appropriate to perform magic during the holy days to Hekate, such as the Deipnon and Noumenia. Generally, devotees set intentions for the month ahead on this day and perform rituals petitioning for Hekate's blessing on their plans.

Exercise: Writing a Noumenia Intentional Prayer

An intentional prayer combines a petition to Hekate with our gratitude, makes a personal commitment to realize our intention and includes magical symbolism. I differentiate between intentional prayers and spells because spells are a lot more work. They usually involve, at least for me, carefully designing a ritual, selecting correspondences and making things including potions and talismans. I also find that intentional prayers are much more intimate than a spell. For me, a spell is an energetic party where I invite herbs, colors and usually the moon in addition to Hekate and myself. That's quite a crowd. An intention prayer is something that's just between me and Hekate. There's no big production number of doing an evocation or full ritual. It's just me and Her, like having late-night conversation with your best friend, who happens to be an all-powerful goddess.

Put time and effort into developing your intention and the text. Think about what you want to accomplish by petitioning Hekate for Her favor in this matter. More importantly, decide what it is you're willing to do to achieve your desired outcome. While this is an intimate discussion, it is not random pillow talk. The intentional prayer is used when you want to make changes in your life. It is a fantastic tool for personal development.

Noumenia is the best day of the lunar cycle for intentional prayer. This is the modern application of the traditional practice of cleaning out the house and seeking Hekate's blessing for the month ahead. In our twenty-first-century world, the house we often need to clean is our internal one. We can be cluttered with dysfunctional thoughts, burdened with fear-based emotions or stuck in bad habits. However, on this day of the New Moon, we can be reborn – or at least begin the process. Each New Moon is a new opportunity for personal development.

I arrange my plans for self-improvement around the Noumenia. I suggest you do the same, whether it's for weight loss, improving a relationship, finding a new job or being kinder to yourself. Feeling that you want to be better is a symptom of living a magical life. The intention needs to be very specific. Think of it as your goal for the upcoming month. It may be a short-term one, such as "give up chocolate for the month" or "stop texting this person." Things that can easily be accomplished in that one lunar cycle. Or it may be part of a long-term goal that will be a process. For example, if you want to change jobs, it's probably not going to happen in the next four weeks, especially if you need to acquire new skills to move into the career you want. Break it down into manageable parts. Start with the first one – it can even be "my intention is to develop a well-thought out actionable plan for _____." Sometimes, that's the best place to start.

Steps in Writing Your Intentional Prayer

Before the Noumenia, contemplate what it is you want to work on during the next lunar phase. Sometimes, this will be obvious, other times you might have to think about it. You certainly don't have to set a lofty goal for the month ahead. It can be simple: "be kinder to my co-workers." Some months your intention might be to continue doing exactly what you've been doing, although in my experience this is rarely the case.

Step 1: Weave a Word Web

In the middle of a fresh page in your journal, write down what it is you want to accomplish. Around this core concept, write the parts of the intention. Draw circles around all these things and connect them. Then around these write the things you can do to achieve each part of the intention. Connect them back to the specific part. Outside of all of this, write the specific types of guidance and intervention that you'd like from Hekate, connecting these to the parts that match up.

Step 2: Choosing Appropriate Aspects of Hekate

We work with Hekate as Guardian, Guide and Gatekeeper. How do each of these relate to the parts of your intention? Add these as circles in your web. Being selective of what aspects of Hekate to involve in any working, not just an intentional prayer, helps to improve the probability of successfully earning Her blessing over any project. She's got a lot on Her plate! If you asked someone for help, but didn't say what you specifically needed, how likely would it be that you'd receive what it was you were hoping for? The same thing works for connecting to Hekate, when we are specific in our requests and in what energy of Hers we want to intervene, then we're much more effective.

Step 3: Writing Your Intention

Using your web, come up with a short intention. It should only be a sentence or two. Make it something that you can reasonably achieve in the next month. Build success into your intention by making it achievable.

Step 4: Make a Plan

Write out the various parts of your plan. Be specific, use deadlines. Consider the aspects of Hekate that you'll be petitioning for help. Once the plan is finished, then it's time to write the prayer.

Step 5: Writing the Prayer

The prayer should be active rather than passive. You should confidently seek out Hekate's attention and favor. Keep it short and to the point. Begin the prayer with exaltation to Hekate, referring to the other prayers you've done so far in this course for guidance in writing this. The exaltation summons Hekate into our presence. Move onto what you are committed to doing and what you are seeking from Hekate. In a spell this is known as the incantation. The final part of the intentional prayer is the same as any working – the dismissal. Finish by expressing gratitude to Hekate for her presence, guidance and protection. The use of a formal dismissal is usually something like "thank you for your attention and I bid you farewell." It probably goes without saying that once you get your prayer finalized, it should go into your Book of Shadows, but I've said it anyway.

Step 6: Saying the Prayer

The prayer should be said after dark on Noumenia, when the first sliver of moon is visible in the night sky. Prepare your altar by lighting a fresh candle. You can light this candle during the month ahead to boost your motivation and Hekate's favor. Stand in front of your altar with your left palm facing down and the right facing up, recite your prayer. It's a good idea to do your daily chanting right before you say the prayer.

Step 7: After the Prayer

It's common that Hekate presents a message during an intention prayer, so be prepared to record it in your journal. Contemplate the message as you need to. Every day – whenever possible – record your progress and signs of Hekate's guidance and intervention.

The intentional prayer doesn't have to be limited to Noumenia. You can use this technique whenever you have a specific project that you want to work on that requires Hekate's support.

Other Days

Any time is fine to honor Hekate. You may feel so grateful that you do a quick ritual thanking Her for a specific blessing. You may want to honor her as a Goddess of the Moon when it's full. Don't feel that you must restrict expressing your devotion to the Deipnon and Noumenia! And your daily chanting is a form of devotion to both Hekate and yourself, so you can add a few special words to that whenever you feel led.

Practice: Affirmations

When we honor Hekate, we often recite exaltations that reflect her positive attributes. Affirmations are the way we honor ourselves saying similar things. A daily practice of reflecting on positive attributes about yourself further deactivates our shadow. Since we work with the Three Selves, you can organize your affirmations into the categories of emotions, thoughts and actions. You can even refer to the epithets we use in this course and use those for your affirmations. The epithets used in the fear and love energy exercise are a great source for this. For example, when you have a difficult day ahead you can say "I am Pyripnoa, the Fire Breather" or remind yourself that you really are quite attractive by saying "I am Kalliste, the Fairest." You can make up a series of affirmation cards from which you can select a few to carry with you as needed. Another idea is to make a list in your journal and reflect upon the energies that each one summons. If you want to manifest your goals, reminding yourself of your strengths helps activate our energies in that direction. It might seem a little goofy at first, but you'll soon see the benefit of practicing them every day as part of your Witch's Hour of Power. Affirmations are a great tool for honoring ourselves. A way I like to work with the three principles is by connecting them to certain epithets that I then make into cards and incorporate into my daily Three Keys Chanting. There's a lot of power in claiming these ancient titles for yourself, especially when saying them in Greek.

Summary

Hekate is honored through offerings, rituals and activities. Offerings can include a variety of things and activities, ranging from traditional ones of fruit to contemporary devotional acts such as community service. Offerings are usually part of a devotional ritual. Our rituals typically start with a petition seeking Our Lady's favor. This can be a simple request right up to a full-scale evocation of Hekate. The process for evoking Hekate requires developing skills and comfort with Her presence. The days associated with honoring Hekate are situated within our understanding of the energies of the different phases of the moon. The Dark Moon, known as the Deipnon is the day set aside by devotees to honor Hekate. The following day when the first sliver of moon is visible is the day to set our intentions for the new lunar phase and seek Hekate's blessing upon them. Honoring ourselves is equally important to our work with Hekate. Some of the ways that we take good care of ourselves are developing a regular gratitude practice and by using affirmations. Both techniques are part of our Witch's Hour of Power.

Lesson 7: Hekate's Wheel of the Year

The Wheel of the Year that most of us are familiar with contains the seasons and sabbats but doesn't involve Hekate in any way. This new Wheel of the Year remedies that situation by incorporating days honoring Hekate into the seasons and months. Having this Wheel of Year is useful for celebrating the sabbats, planning our devotional activities and for the timing of spells. In this lesson, I talk about the development of this wheel, the contents and provide instructions for making your own. The sources for the Wheel were ancient days and festivals, contemporary holy days for Hekate, modern Pagan observances and my interpretations.

Ancient Days and Festivals

The ancient holy days associated specifically with Hekate can be grouped into two categories: every lunar cycle and special events. You've already experienced the Deipnon and Noumenia. For special events, there were three dates set aside to honor Hekate as *Kourotrophos,* Guardian of Children. Those dates correspond to specific phases of the moon cycle. While the ancient calendar is a bit tricky to interpret using our modern one, the dates can be estimated. The days were held on the 27th day of the January-February moon cycle, the third day of June-July moon cycle and the 16th day of August-September moon cycle. You can work with Hekate as the Guardian of Children on any of these dates. A suitable ritual that includes thanking Hekate for the children in your life and seeking her blessing over them is appropriate. In the Wheel of the Year, Hekate as *Kourotrophos* is honored during the August-September moon cycle with a ritual, although you can work with Hekate in this capacity any time you feel led.

Modern Events

The Rite of Her Sacred Fires[31] was developed by Sorita d'Este and others in conjunction with her book of the same name. This event has spread around the world since its inception in 2010.

Hekate's Night is observed on August 13. This is associated with Hekate and storms, which is interesting because none of the ancient texts directly associated Her with the weather. I've always associated Hekate with storms because I erroneously interpreted her epithet of *Brimo* as connected to the weather.[32] Since I made this mistake years ago, Hekate has become associated with storms and with this night by many others. Thus, after dark on August 13, I recommend that you pay your respects to Hekate as the Storm Bringer. You can perform a simple ritual that honors Her for seeing you through the storms of life and seek her guidance for the future ones. If this date happens to be close to the day of Hekate as Guardian of the Children, you can perform a two-fold ritual.

November is recognized as Hekate's Month.[33] The month begins early, with Hekate as a Goddess of Witchcraft being celebrated on Samhain on October 31. On November 1, it is the day to pay homage to our ancestors through rituals honoring them and seeking Hekate's blessing for the dead. In this capacity she is known as Psychopompe or Mistress of Corpses. There are two additional days honoring different aspects of Our Lady. November 16 is a night expressing devotion to Hekate of the Under World.[34] Honoring Hekate as Queen of the Under World is a time for reflection on our personal Under World journeys – those dark nights of the soul – and how Hekate has protected us during those times. Finally, on November 30, the Day of Hekate of the Crossroads is observed.[35] The personal development focus for this celebration is to reinforce your commitment to living your truth. There are times when we come to a crossroads and the easier choice would be to veer off our Witch's Journey to seemingly greener pastures. On the Day of Hekate of the Crossroads envision your life as a series of gates and thresholds, each one with the potential to help us advance. Hekate is there to protect us, but She won't change our course.

The traditional Wheel of the Year begins on November, during the time of Hekate as Guardian which begins in September. The Day of Hekate of the Under World is an appropriate time to honor Her as your Guardian. The Winter Solstice is the day to mark the return of the light, with Hekate as Soteira recognized. A celebration of Hekate as the World Soul occurs on January 1 to kick start the new calendar year. The season of Hekate as Guide begins with the return of the sun on the Winter Solstice. On February 1, Hekate as Guide can be celebrated. Within the traditional Pagan Wheel of the Year this is Imbolc, this time is for honoring Brigit. The symbolism of this Irish Goddess is very much in keeping with Hekate as Guide. Suitable rituals for this date can incorporate Brigit if you wish. In terms of honoring Hekate, a ritual involving fire is appropriate. You want to express gratitude for Her guidance through your journey in this life. In addition, take time to recognize your accomplishments – where you have been your own light, and times that you've shone the light for others. The Spring Equinox is a day for reflecting on Hekate as the Mistress of Balance, as She is represented by the equal length of dark and light. Beltane, occurring at the beginning of May can include Hekate as the Great Mother, Queen of Fire or in a general way with Her World Soul aspect. Finally, Hekate as Gatekeeper is recognized on the Summer Solstice. On the longest day of the year with the bounty of the earth in full bloom, it's time to do a ritual of gratitude.

For the eight days sacred to Hekate that I've mentioned as part of Modern Hekatean Witchcraft, I encourage you to develop your own rituals. You can use the epithets and the correspondences discussed to help with your planning or do something entirely unique. Whatever you feel led to do. The ninth day is the Rite of Her Sacred Fires in May. You can find the information about this event online.

The Sabbats

There are thirteen sabbats – the nine previously discussed plus the four days marking the changing of the seasons. Developing your own ritual for the seasonal changes is an excellent devotional activity. There are additional prayers for you to use, and as a source of inspiration for writing your own in the back of this book, including ones for the Spring Equinox, Summer Solstice, Day of Hekate as Guardian of the Children, Day of Hekate as Storm Bringer, the Fall Equinox, Day of Hekate of the Under World, Day of Hekate as the Goddess of Witchcraft, and the Winter Solstice.

Seasons

In the ancient texts, Hekate was not directly associated with the seasons. However, in the Pagan Wheel of the Year, special attention is paid to the beginning of each new one and the halfway point between them. Hekate's Wheel of the Year incorporates this practice by focusing on aspects of Hekate and/ or energetic symbolism. Hekate's three roles and associated epithets in conjunction with the months and seasons yield a full calendar. The monthly epithets have been chosen to reflect this dominant energy present in the natural world at that time. By calling up Hekate in a form that is closely linked to the natural cycle of the year, we can both honor her and summon the natural energy, resulting in a combined force that produces powerful magic. To use the monthly epithet in a working, you can use it on its own or better yet combine it with two other aspects to create a power triad.

Winter

The calendar year begins with the end of the dominant energy of Hekate as Guardian as it shifts into Hekate as Guide. As January is the beginning of the New Year, Hekate as the World Soul is paid tribute. The energy of the New Year is given a boost by working with Hekate as *Kyria* during February. This epithet connects to Hekate's mighty power which is busy deep in the ground stirring the plants and animals back to life. This shift in the natural energy from the dormancy of early winter is the energy of beginnings. In March, Hekate's dominant energy is as *Ergatis*, referring to her vital powers of creation busily working to manifest the season of spring. On the Spring Equinox, the balance of all things is recognized in Hekate's role as the Mistress of Balance.

Spring

Then in April with the full realization of spring, we celebrate Hekate as *Enodia* at the end of the part of the calendar year devoted to her role as Guide. The glory of the new season is recognized through the energy of Hekate as Glorious Queen, *Kydmios* in the month of May. The seasonal energy of early spring is growth and then moves into abundance in June.

Summer

As the spring moves forward towards summer, Hekate's dominant energy becomes that of Gatekeeper. The symbolism of the key with this season lies in the bounty of the land. We can see that we have traveled through the Under World with the help of Hekate's Light, through the Middle World to a time of plenty. In June, the sun is at its strongest and the earth is the most alive, so Hekate as Goddess of Power, *Kratais,* is seen as the dominant energy. July sees Hekate as *Kleidoukhos*, the universal key bearer and Gatekeeper. August 1 is set aside for honoring Her as the Gatekeeper. Even in such times, Hekate remains as our Guardian, so in August, she is celebrated as *Hegemonen.* For while the sun is still high, and the land is full of plenty, there is the hint that darker days are in the future. The two sabbats this month reflect Her role as Guardian, as the Storm Bringer and as Guardian of the Children.

Fall

The season of Hekate as Guardian becomes fully realized in September when the daylight starts to noticeably wane. The fall is a time of decay and decline when Her keys of growth are removed from the earth. As the daylight hours wane and the veil between worlds thins, She beckons us into the darker mysteries of ourselves and the universe. Black is the color of the fall. As the nights get longer, Hekate's eternal torches burn brighter.

September is the month of Hekate as Guardian, *Lampadios*, and is the time of harvest. The dominant energy of October begins as decay and moves towards death as the veil thins into November. October is the month when the veil between worlds thins and our descent into darkness deepens, reflected in the role of Hekate as *Nykhia*, the Night Wandered Goddess who protects us from evil. For many of us, this month has multiple meanings that culminate in the celebration of Halloween or Samhain on October 31. It is on this day that we can celebrate our witchiness and honor Hekate as our Queen. The next day, November 1, is reserved as a day to pay tribute to our ancestors, whether our actual departed loved ones or others.

November is the month most sacred to Hekate as there are two sabbats in this month. The epithet for November is Chthonia, reflecting Hekate as the Goddess of the Underworld, the day for honoring Hekate as Guardian. Winter is celebrated as the time when the light begins to return. In this manner, Hekate as the Savior from darkness, *Soteira,* is the dominant energy of the month of December. The return of the sun is the dominant theme for December. In our personal development work and spell craft, we can harness the idea of "returning" to create fantastic energy. This is the last epithet associated with Hekate as Guardian for she truly reaches the apex of this aspect on the Winter Solstice.

Lunar Days

As discussed in the last lesson, the Dark Moon is observed as a day to honor Hekate while Noumenia is the day to set our intentions for the month ahead. The Full Moon is the optimal time for spells but can also be used to honor other deities and entities that you work with.

Days of the Week

The final section of our discussion about Hekate's Wheel of the Year concerns the associations between Hekate and the days of the week. There seems to be several different days of the week that have been associated with Hekate in recent years. I've always observed Wednesday as the day of week associated with Hekate for no reason except that I am a Gemini and Wednesday (Mercury's day) is my favorite day of the week. Seriously, Hekate is linked with Mercury in a few ancient texts. For example, "*Brimo* (Hekate), who as legend tells, by the waters of Boebeis laid her virgin body at Mercurius's side" was written by the Roman poet, Propertius.[36] In addition, Mercury is interpreted as the Roman variation of Hermes, who was one of Hekate's frequent collaborators. Monday and Saturday are special to Our Lady as well. She is believed to be linked to Saturn through Her connection to the Moon, although this is a modern interpretation. But that renders Saturday (Saturn's day) and Monday (Moon day) relevant to Hekate.

Exercise: Making Hekate's Wheel of the Year

Using Hekate's Wheel – also known as the strophalos – you can construct a representation of the components of the year discussed in this lesson. I've provided a template of a strophalos divided into twelve segments below that you can photocopy and enlarge to make your Wheel, or you can make your own from scratch using the directions from the lesson on Hekate's Symbols. If you are photocopying this Wheel, I recommend that you use a heavier grade of paper, so it will be more durable. A better technique is to trace the Wheel onto a hard surface, such as a thin piece of wood or an artist's canvas. My sister and I painted the original one on an old window that she rescued from a dumpster.

Figure 1. Hekate's Wheel of the Year Template

Instructions

The Wheel of the Year in the figure is already divided into twelve sections. If you are making your own, this part should be done with a ruler and protractor to ensure that the segments are equally divided. Once you have the blank Wheel ready, you can begin to complete it. Start with the three parts of the coiled serpent. Label each one of them with one of Hekate's Three Roles: Guardian, Guide and Gatekeeper. Next, label each of the months on the outside of the big circle (this represents Hekate) in conjunction with how you labeled each of the serpent's coils. You can use the monthly themes I used or choose your own. Then in the space between Hekate's Circle and the serpent's coils write the name of each of the seasons in the corresponding location. Add the months next and then choose an epithet that represents the energy of that month to you. Using a lunar calendar, you can add the dates for the thirteen Dark Moons, New Moons and Full Moons. The final touch should be adding the personal days that are important to you, like birthdays and anniversaries. This yields a Wheel of the Year with 39 (plus your personal ones) days, a number reflecting Hekate in Her three-fold form.

Blessing of Hekate's Wheel of the Year

The Wheel that you've created is part of your sacred space. It can be used as a backdrop behind the salt strophalos that you created. Since it is a sacred object that you'll use in devotion and witchcraft, it needs to be consecrated. Place the Wheel near your existing altar components of the salt strophalos, your statement and image of Hekate. Using the daily chant, clear your mind of thoughts. Once you are in this altered state, recite the blessing over your Wheel:

> Hail Hekate, Goddess of All Creation,
> Ruler of the natural cycles of the earth,
> Who reigns over time
> Bless the Wheel of the Year
> May the days of my life
> Be forever under your guidance,
> Bless the Wheel of the Year,
> And all
> The days,
> The weeks,
> The months,
> The sabbats,
> And the seasons
> Of my life.
> Hail Hekate, Goddess of All Creation,
> Ruler of the natural cycles of the earth.

NB: You can adapt this blessing for use on just about any object that you want to consecrate. Just change the wording to reflect what you're doing. Also, I always use "And so it is!" at the end of a working as appropriate. You can end a working however you like. For example, using "Blessed Be" is entirely suitable.

Practice: Automatic Writing

I recommend getting a separate notebook from your journal for automatic writing. While studying the Wheel have your notebook and pen ready. Begin with the month that you are in currently. Say the name of the month and the epithet associated with it. You may need to do this a few times to get into the energy of the Wheel. After you've chanted this at least three times, images associated with the month will start to appear in your mind's eye. Ignore them. Instead let your pen start writing. This technique will reveal Hekate's messages for you for that month. While you certainly can work through multiple months or even the entire calendar during one session, it's my experience that this can be quite exhausting. A better approach is to schedule a "monthly update" that is part of the beginning of a calendar month. After the automatic writing stops (it will end when Hekate is done delivering her guidance for the calendar month), take time to process her messages by writing about them in your journal.

Practice: Establishing a Deipnon and Noumenia Monthly Practice

There are three powerful symbols used in Modern Hekatean Witchcraft, they include Hekate's Fire, Wheel and Key. Before we commence a detailed review of these symbols, I want to congratulate you on reaching this part of the course. Now that you've completed your first cycle of the moon after your initial Deipnon and Noumenia rituals, it's time to start your own monthly practice of these events. The Deipnon can be a very simple ritual with an offering and a few works to Hekate. Noumenia intention setting should reflect what you hope to achieve in the coming month. Sometimes my Noumenia intention is for things to remain the same.

Summary

Hekate's Wheel of the Year is an amalgamation of Hekate's

roles and epithets, ancient festival days, the modern pagan calendar, and the nature's cycles. There are thirteen special days – or sabbats – included in the calendar. Twelve are devoted to aspects of Hekate and the natural cycles and the thirteenth is your birthday. On each sabbat we celebrate different aspects of Hekate and ourselves. The calendar year is divided into Hekate as Guardian, Guide and Gatekeeper with seasonal and monthly associations. Finally, the three days of the week associated with Hekate are Wednesday, Saturday and Monday. Making your own Wheel of the Year is a great way to study the sabbats and other special days. The new technique introduced in association with the Wheel of the Year is automatic writing, where you channel messages through intense focus on the Wheel.

Lesson 8: Hekate's Symbols

Hekate's three main symbols are keys, fire and the strophalos, commonly known as Hekate's Wheel.

Keys

Hekate as Kleidoukhos is the Keeper of the Keys. This understanding of Our Lady has become a very popular image with contemporary devotees. While the *Orphic Hymn* assigns Her this epithet, there are few other ancient references to Her in this role. The story about a girl carrying a key to open the temple at Lagina, the last known temple to Hekate, is one of my favorites.

Contemporary Hekate's Key Symbolism

Perhaps it makes sense for our modern interpretation of Hekate to be so strongly associated with such a ubiquitous item as the key. We have lots of keys – to our home, our car, our office. We use another form of key: passwords, for accessing just about everything on our devices. Keys are everywhere. And if you're asking me, I'm going to say that Hekate is everywhere, too.

I have lots of keys – antique ones, old ones, wooden ones, and even a beautiful diamond and white gold necklace that was a gift from my sweet mother. Key symbolism is so powerful. We associate getting a key with starting something new. In addition, we use keys in the form of passwords to gain access to things we hold dear, from our Facebook account to our mailbox. We use the word "key" as an adjective to signify that something is important – "my key point is ...," for example. Key is also a verb: "the key to figuring this out ..." We use them symbolically, like "Keeping Her Keys." When I chose this name for the blog, it was because of the dual meaning. I'm keeping Hekate's Keys – at least the ones She has given me, and I'm keeping my own keys –

meaning that I am living life on my terms. There are many ways to use keys in witchcraft. I often infuse keys with intentions in spells in the same way my sacred keys are expressions of my thanks for Hekate's many gifts.

Instant Key Magic

One of the keys that Hekate has given me is the key to witchcraft. There are so many uses for actual keys in witchery. The fantastic thing about using keys for magical purposes (I'm including both devotion and witchcraft in this) is that we have easy access to them. If we wanted to do a spell for house protection, there is no better place to park the magical energy of our intention into our house key. This is one of my favorite go-to's for instant magic. I hold the key that represents my focus and zap my intention into it. No need to consecrate the key because its existing energy is exactly what I want.

Using Keys to Express Devotion to Hekate

Beyond this sort of quickie witchery, there are countless ways to use keys in devotion and magic. Many devotees display keys as part of their shrine or altar as a representation of Our Lady. I have one very special antique skeleton key that has been in my family for a long time that is always on my altar. It's both a symbol of Hekate and a small way of honoring my ancestors. We can charge our keys with our gratitude to Hekate using a simple ritual where we give the key back to Her. Or we can simply use them as decorations.

Hekate's Wheel

There are many ways to incorporate the strophalos into witchcraft. My two favorite ways are by making strophaloi as an energetic focal point or by using the strophalos to create sacred space for witchcraft and devotion because of its intense symbolic energy. We can look to the origins of the strophalos for an explanation of why it is so powerful. The connection of the strophalos to Hekate is often viewed as stemming from a passage in *The Chaldean Oracles*. The strophalos is seen as containing the serpent of life. In antiquity, strophaloi (the plural) were spinning tools (iynx) used in rituals or spells. Sort of an ancient magical fidget spinner. There are many different theories as to its origin story and how it was used in ancient times and there is no direct connection between Hekate and Her Wheel found in the historical record. However, this contemporary connection has become strongly associated with Our Lady.

Parts of the Strophalos

The complex meaning of the strophalos is revealed by looking at its components. The strophalos consists of an outer circle. I like to think of this great circle as Hekate as the World Soul, representing Her as Creatrix and as the mediator between us and the universe. Immediately inside this circle is the labyrinthine design of the serpent that is the life force of all things. It also can signify birth and rebirth. After the snake, there is another circle. This circle represents our sovereignty. We are connected to the life force and to Hekate but are also individuals. Encapsulated within this circle is a six-pointed figure with another circle at its center. To me, this represents the divine within us. This six-pointed figure can be interpreted in at least three different ways: a star, a sun, or even a flower. The flower interpretation comes from *The Chaldean Oracles* reference to Hekate as the fiery rose (flower) of creation. The star is also symbolic of Hekate of the Under World with the starlight representing Her torches and the night sky as dark energy. The sun is the opposite energy current, with Hekate in Her Upper World aspects. Thus, the six-pointed figure is also a tripartite representation of Hekate. The strophalos contains three circles. The snake is in three coils. Given that this yields three groups of three, it's no wonder the strophalos is viewed as such a powerful symbol of witchcraft.

The strophalos today is often seen as an image of devotion to Hekate and a symbol of witchcraft. Images are often seen as personal declarations of devotion and witchery. Some people have Hekate's Wheel tattoos, for example.

Using the Strophalos as a Sacred Symbol

With its three circles, three coils, and threefold meaning of the central figure, the strophalos provides endless magical possibilities. I've used each of the different coils to represent things I am grateful for, and to represent different aspects of my life for which I am seeking Hekate's help, petitioning Hekate using the threefold meaning of the central figure. You can assign components of a spell onto the different parts of the strophalos, infusing them as you do with your intention and petitioning Hekate to bless each bit.

The Energy of Hekate's Wheel

In addition to the powerful symbolic energy of the strophalos that I've already written about, there is also the motion of the wheel to consider. As a spinning object, it can be used to send out energy (clockwise) or to attract energy (counter clockwise). Envisioning this spinning energy as creating waves that not only go out horizontally but also in every other possible direction led me to the idea that the strophalos would be a fantastic way to create a sacred space.

Exercise: Making a Strophalos

You can make a strophalos to use as a symbolic representation of Hekate and Her energies, as a magical coin on its own or in a talisman, or even create a giant one as a sacred space. I'm going to go over the process for making one for your altar, but if you want to make an additional one to wear or for use as a magical coin, you can follow the same steps. If you're doing this, there are lots of great different types of hardening compounds out there to use. If you're not sure how to use these products, check out the multitude of YouTube videos. You can also paint one on a rock, shell or other small surface.

Strophalos Making: A Step-by-Step Guide

There are so many ways to create a strophalos. I'm going to describe how to make one using a template and then move onto the creation of a salt strophalos for use in cleansing magical objects.

Using a Template

I have a template that I created using circular objects, a ruler, and a protractor. You can do the same or photocopy the one in the section on Hekate's Wheel and enlarge it to the size you need. Once I made this original, I then traced over it using parchment paper. With the strophalos on parchment, I can trace it again onto just about any surface. I have used a very sharp craft knife (my version of a magical blade) to cut out the shape of the strophalos after I've traced it onto the parchment. Another way to transfer the image onto another surface is by using a semi-blunt pointy thing to copy over the parchment template. This will leave an impression on the surface the strophalos is being transferred onto. Once you've got that template, you can transfer it onto lots of things but for this exercise, you'll be using it as a reference for making the strophalos for your altar.

Making a Salt Strophalos for Cleansing Objects and Tools

While there are many ways that you can construct your own strophalos for your altar, I am going to discuss a very specific type – a salt strophalos. Salt is a great energetic source to use in magic because it is both protective and easily adaptable. You can charge salt with just about any sort of intention. We'll be using this salt strophalos for preparing magical objects throughout the course, although you can use it in other ways.

What You'll Need

- An unpainted wooden tray with sides that are at least one inch high. I recommend that the tray be at least 8x10 inches. You should use one that will fit on your altar, with room to spare for the additional things that you'll be adding later. You can use just about any type of wooden tray – a shallow box or even a deep-sided picture frame will work.
- Enough salt (preferably sea) to cover the tray. The actual amount depends on the size of the tray.
- Narrow pointy thing, like a thin paintbrush or even a nail file.
- A toothpick.
- Black cloth or black paint to cover the interior of the tray.
- Two circles, one about one-third the diameter of the other. The larger one should fit just inside the frame. You can use a small paint can and a jar top, for example.

Directions

After unwrapping your strophalos components ask Hekate to bless the objects and your work with them. Make sure you have your strophalos template on hand, so you can look at it while you construct your salt one. The next step is to either paint the inside of the tray or cover it with a black cloth. Once this is done (and the paint is dry), spread the salt out evenly on the inside of the tray to about a half- inch thickness. Using the larger circular object, press it into the salt until a circle is formed. Remove the object. You can also trace around the circle using your skinny pointy thing. You should see the outer circle representing Hekate. Next position the small circle in the middle of the larger one. Repeat the process until you have another circle, representing you. Inside this circle, draw the six rays by constructing three crossing lines. I used the end of a slender paintbrush to do this, if your strophalos is smaller, you can use a toothpick.

Now we're at the part that seems really complicated but isn't once it's broken down into the components. Think of the interior figure as a three-coiled serpent representing all the three energetic realms. Think of the serpent as six lines, arcs really, that are drawn – three each – around the middle circle and inside the outer circle. Try to think of it this way when you're drawing it rather than thinking about each coil. It's much easier to conceptualize this way. Three arcs go around the central circle and three just inside the outer circle. There is a gap between each arc that's about one-third of the length of each arc.

Next, find the midpoint of one of the first series of arcs. Extend this down to just outside the central circle. Eyeball it and you won't have to erase lines! Use this as your starting point for the first arc outside of the central circle. Extend this arc to the midpoint of the next outer arc. Leave a gap and repeat this process for two more arcs. You end up with three arcs just inside the outer circle and three arcs just outside the central circle. The gap between each arc in each set is about the midpoint of an arc in the other set. Finish connecting the inner arcs to the outer ones by linking the end points of the lines to the adjacent ones. The serpent is made up of two sets of three arcs and six connectors. Now that the strophalos is complete, place it on your altar. After it's in position, say the Hekate's Wheel prayer over it. As you recite the prayer, focus your attention on the part of the strophalos that you are describing. Visualize the energy of each part. This will help charge the strophalos with energy, consecrating for use in your rituals and spells.

Strophalos Blessing

Hail Hekate, Guardian,
Hail Hekate, Guide,

Hail Hekate, Gatekeeper.

Attend me now,

As I consecrate this Wheel for use in Your name.

I am the center, with my soul my core,

I reach out from my six rays connecting to the world around
me.

And to You, Mighty Hekate.

I exist within the circle of my own sovereignty,

My individuality and free will.

I am surrounded by the realms of the three-coiled serpent.

The depths of the Under World,

The heights of the Upper World,

And the balanced plane of the Middle World,

All are Your creation,

As you encircle all things, Mighty Hekate.

Bless this strophalos for my magical workings,

May my intent be true,

My actions wise

And my will strong.

Accept my gratitude for Your presence,

Hail Hekate, Guardian,

Hail Hekate, Guide,

Hail Hekate, Gatekeeper.

You can adapt this blessing to use when preparing other objects for magical uses or leave out the parts specific to consecrating the Wheel and use it as an all-purpose prayer.

Hekate's Fire

I've already mentioned that Hekate is explained as the fire of creation in *The Chaldean Oracles*. Here's the fragment: "… from there, a lightning-bolt, sweeping along, obscures the flower of fire as it leaps into the hollows of the worlds. For from there, all things begin to extend wonderful rays down below." Given that Hekate is the fire of creation, all other types of fire are an extension of her one source-fire. Hekate is certainly a Queen of Fire. The four other types of fire I'll be discussing are: stars, torches, lamps and our soul-fire.

Hekate and Stars

Hekate's association with stars is found in *The Chaldean Oracles* and *The Greek Magical Papyri (PGM)* and other ancient sources. An invocation spell in the *PGM* refers to her as walking among the stars:

Lamp-bearer, shining and aglow, Selene, Star-coursing, heavenly, torch-bearer, fire-breather ... (IV, 2557). [Note: In the *PGM*, Hekate is syncretized with other goddesses including Selene.]

In ancient times stars were mysterious sources of energy. Different numbers of stars were associated with different deities, types of power, and other things. Hekate as always was associated with the number three, but also with seven.

Hekate's Torches

In ancient rituals, spells and tales, Hekate is seen as lighting the way with her blazing torches. Perhaps the most commonly known is The *Homeric Hymn to Demeter* where Hekate's torches light Persephone's way to and from the Under World. Images of Hekate holding her torches can be found in ancient representations of her, including magical coins. My personal perception of Hekate tends to see her as holding one lamp, rather than any number of torches. It doesn't matter what type of fire she uses to light our way. There are several ancient references to Hekate as *Lampadios* (lamp-bearer), including the example I quoted earlier.

Our Soul-Fire

Another application of torch-bearer symbolism is that we hold the light to our own way, perhaps bestowed upon us by Hekate herself. Taking this idea further is the idea that we hold within our soul a spark of Hekate's creation fire.

Using Fire in Devotion and Magic

Many modern Hekateans include lamps on their altars, while others have two flames (usually candles) that symbolize her twin torches. Unlike keys and Hekate's Wheel, the lamp (or torch) is a symbol firmly resting in Hekate's hand. We can hold a strophalos or key in our own hands, imbue these symbols with our own energy, intentions, and invoke Hekate's energy into them. The torch is a very different type of symbol. We typically use it to represent Hekate rather than as a magical tool. However, candle magic can be interpreted as a tool of Hekate's fire when we involve her in our rituals and spells. However, we choose to use Hekate's fire in our personal practice, her potent energy is sure to accompany our magic.

Hekate's Fires and the Three Realms

I find it helpful to organize the different types of flames according to their properties using the three energetic realms. All fires flow from Hekate's fire of creation, so they are all part of that original fire. The torch is the symbol of the Under World, lighting the darkness and providing guidance, as Hekate did for Persephone. The Upper World is represented by the fiery energy of the stars. In the Middle World, Hekate's lamp lights the way through our earth-bound journey. All three realms are connected through their individual fire energy. Hekate's torches led Persephone back to the Middle World after her time with Hades, connecting these two realms. The fire of the Upper World gave birth to the material Middle World. When I do a journey with Hekate as a guide, she shines her lamp as I travel within the Upper World and Under World.

Hekate's Fire Symbolism

I've focused on Hekate's fires as sources of light that guides us in a variety of different ways in this aspect she is very much a Goddess of Light. I also mentioned the power of her sacred fire of creation. I see the fires I use in my own witchcraft in a similar way – I often use fires as a tool of manifestation. In addition, I use fire in the way that many people see it – as a tool of destruction. For example, if I wish to release the past, I may write down a few words about this painful memory and then burn the paper. Beyond using actual fire in magic, many modern witches use candles as symbols of both aspects of fire. We use various techniques involving fire energy in our candle magic. Often, we use candles when we create sacred space.

Practice: Fire Scrying

Fire scrying is a time-honored practice used in many different forms of witchcraft. The basic technique is to enter an altered state and then focus your attention on the fire. You're already well prepared to enter an altered state by this point in our course; you can use the counting technique or chanting. You want to be in a light trance where you are open to metaphysical forces but are still aware of your surroundings. I suggest using a black candle, although a white candle will work in a pinch. I also suggest doing this separate from the Deipnon or a sabbat. Noumenia is an ideal time to do divination work for the month ahead.

The room should be dimly lit, to minimize distractions. Light the candle on your altar prior to beginning your chanting. While you light the candle, say something like, "Fire, fire burning bright, grant me insight on this night." If you have a specific issue that you want to explore, concentrate on that. If not, open your awareness.

Instead of closing your eyes, look slightly above the candle while chanting. Take note of any images that come up and record them in your journal. The combination of the sacred flame with your chanting can lead to strong visions coming through. By looking slightly above the candle, we shift our attention away from the direct flame to the energetic field that surrounds the candle. Images will begin to form in the candle itself and extend to the energy field around it. Don't be concerned if images don't appear instantly, remain relaxed and they will come. If your mind starts to wander, dismiss your thoughts by telling them that you'll see them later. If you're new to fire scrying do this exercise for about five minutes. When you are finished, thank the fire for lending its energy to your work. Be sure to journal about the experience. You may also want to record the technique in your Book of Shadows.

Exercise: Using Hekate's Symbols

Keys are a huge part of our modern lives. We may not think that Hekate's Wheel and Her fires are to be found in normal activities, but if we develop our observation skills, we can become better at seeing them. Start recording in your journal whenever you see one of Her symbols in an unexpected place or used in a way that implies that the symbol is a message from Hekate.

Connecting to Hekate's Symbols

After you've been recording your observations of Hekate's symbols for a week or so, you'll start to notice that one of them is more common. It may be Her Keys, Wheel or Fire. You may also have a powerful experience with one or more of the symbols, like finding a key unexpectedly. If you don't already have an idea which of Her symbols is being presented to you as the dominant one for your personal work, you can review your journal to look for patterns. Which one appears the most frequently? Which one seems the most meaningful? While it's natural for us to have one symbol that we hold above the other two, this isn't always the case. It's a good idea to develop an understanding of the energy of all three. To do this, you should explore different representations of keys, the strophalos and Hekate's Fires (i.e., stars, torches and lamps). Keep a record of the various images that you use. You can save them on your device or print them off. One thing I do is print images and construct a Witch Board that contains different elements of my current explorations.

Summary

The three major symbols Hekate are keys, Hekate's Wheel and Hekate's Fires. Keys have powerful symbolic meaning and energy because they are such a part of everyday life and because they are connected to Hekate. The strophalos, also known as Hekate's Wheel, is an ancient magical tool that is now closely linked to Hekate. Finally, Hekate's Fires are represented through Her connections with stars, torches and lamps. We can use the power of fire to receive messages from Hekate and for divinatory work. Learning to notice Hekate's symbols helps develop our skills of observation, which are vital in all energy work, including rituals and spells.

Lesson 9: Correspondences

The realms, epithets and symbols should be very familiar by now, and you might recall that I briefly touched on the dominant energies of each of the three selves in an earlier. I also discussed the varying energy in the lunar cycle. As we progress toward the lesson on spell crafting, I want you to start thinking about how things fit together. Everything we do in witchcraft is based on working with energy. We can add different epithets of Hekate, symbols and correspondences as ways of amplifying the power of the spell.

Preparing Objects for Use as Correspondences

It's important to prepare objects used as correspondences before involving them in a working. Basic preparation includes cleansing each object of any existing non-essential energies and consecrating it for magical purposes. We cleanse objects to release energies that aren't associated with the specific symbolic powers of the object. For example, if I am using a new crystal in a spell then I want to remove the energy of all the people who have handled it while it made its way to me while protecting its inherent magical properties. There are a variety of methods for cleansing objects, such as leaving them outside under the Full Moon, placing them in a jar of magical water or smoking them over incense. Salt is a powerful medium for releasing non-essential energies. Since you've already created your Salt Strophalos, you can place your objects on this to cleanse them. Most objects will be sufficiently cleansed after a few days, especially if you've put them in there during the Full Moon. When you place an object for cleansing, say something like, "You are cleansed of all that's past, free to release your magic at last." You'll need to check-in with the salt to determine when it is full of these unwanted energies and then change it. How long this takes really depends on how much non-essential energy that the correspondence objects you've cleansed in the strophalos have.

The second part of object preparation is to consecrate the item for magical use. You'll be able to tell that an object is ready to leave the salt by picking it up. It will feel clean and you'll have a connection to it. When this happens, take the object and pass it through the smoke from incense several times. I usually do this in multiples of three. You can recite something like this: "I hereby claim this object for my magical workings. May Hekate bless it and me. My intentions are true, my actions wise and my will is strong." Your object is ready for use as a correspondence.

Using Daily and Seasonal Correspondences

The seasons and the days discussed can be sources of energy used in spells and rituals as well. The days of the week more strongly associated with Hekate are based on historical documents, thus we are tapping into an established energetic connection when we seek her attention on Mondays, Wednesdays or Fridays. We can further strengthen this source of energy by unpacking the meaning of these days both in standard interpretations and personal meaning. Since Wednesday is Mercury's Day, I may call upon him as well as Hekate when doing a working.

The seasons also have distinct energies that reflect Hekate's different aspects. We can use the energy of a season as a theme for the type of working we are going to do. For example, you might remember that I discussed the overarching energy of the fall as being that of decay. If we want to cast a spell using this correspondence, then we word it so that whatever our goal is utilizes decay.

Personal Change and Correspondences

Most spellwork has an inherent component of personal change. The process by which this personal change is accomplished consists of four steps: problem, intention, goal and manifestation.

We cast a spell and then get busy manifesting using our feelings, thoughts and behaviors. In addition, most spells are problem-focused. Once we identify the problem, we set the intention for the solution; within this intention is a clearly defined goal that will lead us to successful manifestation. In addition, we can see that the spell components have energies of their own that can be used with the correspondences including the lunar cycle, seasons and colors.

With her three millennia of history, there is a lengthy list of items that we can choose for correspondences in our devotion and witchcraft involving Hekate. Correspondences include animals, plants, minerals and rocks and other things that share energetic properties.

Hekate's Companions

Other deities and entities can also be used as correspondences. I've already mentioned Mercury, who in the Greek pantheon was Hermes, who happens to be a frequent companion of Hekate's. There are many others including Demeter, Persephone, Artemis, Diana and Zeus. Hekate is strongly associated with both angels and daemons. Of course, if you already have a relationship with another deity or have a spirit companion, then include them in your workings as you deem suitable.

Combining Correspondences

When we combine correspondences, we add oomph to our workings. Combining things that have common attributes with Hekate in general or those that are related to specific epithets can make for potent magic. We can also use correspondences in our devotional activities. Sometimes we pick correspondences for a certain spell or ritual, other times there are correspondences that we include on our altar. These objects can change based on our focus, the time of the year or lunar cycle and ways that we work with Hekate. I've developed a list of correspondences that can be used for all these things. I use it as a reference for when I'm planning a ritual or spell. Making your own list either in your Book of Shadows or as a spreadsheet (my method) will help you to understand all the connections better. Don't forget to add your own ones beyond the standards.

Sources

The correspondences I discuss in this lesson come from ancient sources whenever possible, but I've added contemporary ones and some of my own interpretations to incorporate contemporary areas of witchcraft.

Correspondences and Hekate's Three Roles

I've organized correspondences using Hekate's three overarching roles as Guardian, Guide and Gatekeeper. Correspondences of Hekate as Guardian include dogs, black obsidian, the waning moon, sage and the color black. Hekate as Guide can be associated with horses, red jasper, bay laurel and the color red. Snakes, clear quartz, mugwort and the color white are representative of Hekate as Gatekeeper.

Hekate's Animals

There are several animals associated with Hekate in the ancient sources, including bees, bulls, cows, dogs, dragons, goats, horses, lions, owls, pigs, polecats and snakes.[37] Although there are many animal companions of Hekate, the three key ones are dogs, horses and snakes. There are examples of her as *Triformis*, having a dog, horse and serpent head.[38] These are the three animals that we are working with as correspondences in this course. In the ancient texts she is described by some as possessing either one, two or all three of these animals in her physical form, while in other sources she is associated with them. Dogs, horses and snakes are worked with in different ways. Hounds accompany Hekate as Guardian in the Under World, representing emotional energy and loyalty. Horses are her companion as our guardian in her role as Guide, bringing action and stability to our life's journey. Finally, Hekate's Serpents are the potent facilitator of rebirth and knowledge as part of Hekate as the Key of the Upper World.

Working with Animal Energy

Working with animal energy is a potent type of magic. There are several ways that we can tap into animal energy: we can identify with an animal as a spirit guide, we can take on the energetic properties typical of an animal, they can serve as Hekate's messengers, we can use animal energies in spells, and we can evoke them during workings. I have summarized dogs, horses and snakes as they fit into Modern Hekatean Witchcraft. I recommend learning more about them, so you can develop your own personal understanding of your connections to each of them.

Hekate's Hounds

Of these three, perhaps the dog is the best known of Hekate's animal companions. In her ancient cults, dogs were associated with her as companions and they were offered to her as sacrifices. Her 'hell-hounds' guarded the gates to the Under World.[39] She is also viewed as having a canine form herself in some of the writings, either as a single dog or even as a triple-headed one. Black dogs were symbolic of Hekate in ancient times, like in this section from "Spell to the Waning Moon" in *The Greek Magical Papyri: "Her fillet, key, wand, iron wheel, black dog."* Hounds are of special importance in Her role as Guardian, when they offer protection from those who would harm us. Dog energy is particularly emotional as well, reinforcing the placement of this animal as a correspondence of Hekate as Guardian.

Dogs are often sent as a sign by Hekate to modern devotees. In addition, some devotees volunteer time at dog shelters as a devotional act of service, replacing the sacrifice of old with a modern approach. Personally, I've had a couple of experiences with black dogs appearing unexpectedly during rituals. Be on the lookout for one! If one shows up, be prepared to receive a message from Hekate.

There are other magical ways that we can access the Under World energy of Hekate's Hounds in addition to their role as spontaneous messengers. As our companion through our personal Under World, we can call upon them as protectors. We can utilize their terrifying energy when we need to summon our own inner ferocity. Although Hekate's Hounds are fearsome, they are also incredibly loyal and steadfast. If we need sustainable energy for a working, we can evoke these attributes as part of the correspondences used. Hekate's Hounds stand guard at the entrance to the realm of the Under World and to our own lower self. As you become familiar with them, you'll see they are your greatest allies against your own fears. When you are afraid, you can turn to them for protection. Hekate shares the energy of the hounds with us abundantly.

There are numerous ways to connect with the energy of Hekate's Hounds. I have a coyote jaw that I use whenever I am working with dog energy. You may have your own dog – I don't right now, although I've had dogs my entire life – and you can connect to the mystical hounds of Hekate through your alignment with your pet. In addition, you can use your own dog's hair and nails to connect with Hekate's Hounds. If you don't have bones or an actual dog, then you can use dog images or statuary.

Hekate's Horses

Years ago, while I was giving a healing session to a person dying from cancer, I received this powerful vision of a gorgeous wild black horse. At the time I didn't know that Hekate was historically linked with the equine species. Since then I have had a few other visions of horses, but it's always been associated with loss. From the ancient texts we learn that Hekate's horses were like my visions – they were part of Her Under World entourage. They were powerful magical symbols that were evoked as part of Hekate during rituals. In addition, some ancient incantations referred to Her as "horse faced."

Although Hekate's horses were portrayed this way, they were also the domestic work animals that they were and remain. Horses are placed alongside Hekate as Guide. She rides astride the horse as she guides us throughout our life's journey. Hekate's Horse is our reliable companion, capable of great speed, mighty in endurance and very reliable. The energy of the horse is very much about action and representative of the mundane Middle World, further reinforcing this animal's position as a correspondence of the key of Guide. Call upon Hekate's Horse when you need swift magical results or when you feel alone. When working with Hekate's Horse we can use images, parts of the animal (that they are no longer in need of!) or horse shoes on our altars and in our workings.

Hekate's Serpents

While many of us are terrified of snakes, they are powerful symbols of creation and destruction. As such, they are mighty correspondences that we can summon for our magical workings. Hekate's association with serpents is ancient – there are several references connecting Her with them in ancient texts, most prolifically in *The Greek Magical Papyri*. A Roman plaque of a three-headed Hekate with a snake on either side is a popular image today. I've heard Her referred to as a snake goddess which seems highly appropriate since the serpent is like Hekate, a universal symbol of life and death, has countless meanings, and is both vilified and revered. Perhaps the snake is Her most potent animal symbol.

There are so many vivid images of Hekate with snakes in the

ancient texts: having a crown of snakes, being girthed in them, and wearing them down Her back are three examples. Clearly, snakes are in Her favour. As we learn about Hekate's mysteries we realize that snakes are not to be feared but are powerful Upper World allies. They provide much wisdom and are a reminder that all things have the potential for danger. Perhaps more importantly, they show us that we can "shed our skin" and be born anew. Thus, the snake and the key are powerfully connected.

I see an unexpected snake visitor as a very good omen. My experience is that Hekate sends snake's as messengers when we are likely to be too self-involved to notice the less startling hounds or horses that she sends. Each time I've had a snake encounter, one has literally crossed my path. Once there was one in my driveway when I lived in a very urban area! Although our relationships with Hekate's animals are all very special, to me, the snake is very special to me. Serpents remind me that there is duality in all things – from creation to destruction. Moreover, snakes are exceptionally clever animals. Their powerful intelligence is reflected in two ancient symbols – the caduceus and the ouroboros. The former is the well-known symbol of medicine, with two snakes wrapped around a central pole. This is an ancient talisman of healing and power, associated with Hekate's frequent companion, Hermes. The ouroboros is associated with Hekate both in ancient texts and objects, including several magical coins. These coins were used as a manifestation tools. I've made several of these coins for use in my own spells and to carry as talismans. The image of the snake eating her own tail teaches us that all life is circular. Through the infinity of the ouroboros we can connect with Hekate as the Key of the universe, infinite and eternal.

Hekate's Serpent is complex, as you can see from the various aspects that I've just written about. This is why I referred to snakes as her most potent animal. Snakes are associated with her in diverse ways, reflecting Hekate's multi-faceted nature. We are focusing on their Upper World energies of creation. Imagery appropriate for this approach to her serpent includes the ouroboros. I encourage you to read more about this symbol and study the ancient images to truly connect with this form of Hekate's Serpent. I made a golden serpent ouroboros out of polymer clay that I currently work with. In the past, I've used snake skins in workings. My favorite piece of jewelry is a three-coiled silver snake ring. Find your way through serpent energy to the images that you can connect with. As a symbol of the Upper World, call upon Hekate's Serpents when you seek enlightenment, need to release things, or for intellectual pursuits.

Hekate's Colors

While there are other colors associated with Hekate, none are as central to Modern Hekatean Witchcraft as black, red and white. Our Lady is also associated with gold and yellow. She is often described as golden or as wearing golden sandals. There is an ancient connection of her with saffron, giving us the association with this shade of yellow. We can use gold as the color to symbolize Hekate as the World Soul; blue in the form of sapphires and her watery aspects. Green as the color of Her garden is another hue representing Hekate. You can also have a personal color that you associate with Her, for me it's the regal color of purple. The association of black, red and white with Hekate dates to antiquity:

The symbols of Hecate are wax of three colors,
white and black and red combined, having a figure of
Hecate bearing a scourge, and torch, and sword, with
a serpent to be coiled round her.[40]

These three colors were generally seen back then as they are today: as the colors of witchcraft. Black is associated with Hekate as Guardian in her Under World role, while white reflects the Key of Hekate in the Upper World. The two colors come together not to make grey, but red in the Middle World where Hekate is Guide. This framework is based on the historical associations of these colors with the three realms. Black as the color of Hekate as Guardian reflects our emotions and lower self, while white is used to connect to our higher self and Hekate as the Key. Red, the color of the life force symbolized with blood, comes together in the Middle World land of action. I always have black, red and white on my altars and in my workings. Beyond these three colors, there are many ways of incorporating a hue into your magic, as shown in the following list.

Color	Uses
Black	Banishing; mediumship; protection (sending away); reversal
White	Psychic development; protection (attracting); purification
Red	Creativity; passion; romance; sexuality
Orange	Career; children; education; relationships
Yellow	Assertiveness; confidence; self-esteem
Pink	Compassion; happiness; kindness; love
Green	Attracting objects and possessions; abundance; finances; money; major purchases
Blue	Training; talking; teaching; thoughts; writing
Purple	Self-control; connection to the deities and other entities; integrity
Brown	Grounding; land and property
Silver	Use as a symbol of the unified self
Gold	Symbolizes the combination of all Hekate's aspects

Practice: The Witch's Wardrobe

We can practice practical magic with the accessories and clothes that we wear using the list of color correspondences. You can wear blue to a job interview to enhance your skills at communicating what a fantastic employee you'll be, for example. I typically choose a scarf that represents the dominant energy that I'm embracing for the day ahead. You can also choose jewelry using metals and stones that correspond to your intention for the day. Try this out for a week and note your results in your journal. Ancient texts feature Hekate wearing gold sandals, so if you really want to tap into your inner goddess, you know what to wear.

Exercise: Adding Color to the Wheel of the Year

Now that you've learned the three main colors of Modern Hekatean Witchcraft and the energetic properties of several others, you can add to your Wheel of the Year as you feel led.

Exercise: Experiencing the Energy of Hekate's Colors

The Prayer to Hekate, The World Soul was written as part of a devotional project undertaken by The Covenant of Hekate. I was honored to write the prayer in conjunction with the beautiful painting entitled *Mediterranean Hekate*. The prayer has been translated into other languages which I think is very cool. The whole project was such a lovely experience. You can find the painting on my blog if you want to look at it while you recite. I've included this prayer here because of how the colors are used to connect with different aspects of ourselves and Hekate, providing you with an example of how we can link correspondences to epithets and personal attributes. It also demonstrates how we can use words as representations of correspondences rather than the actual objects. I think that words are the most powerful expression of magic, but then I'm a writer so I may have a biased opinion. However, words can link correspondences, intentions, personal attributes and Hekate's energy in a very potent way. I know this prayer has already found a place in many practitioners' Book of Shadows. I recommend that you include it in yours, too.

By now you've got the skills to prepare for saying the prayer, so I won't go over the steps. Feel free to embellish the prayer, add physical representations of the correspondences and develop a ritual around it as you feel led.

Prayer to Hekate, Soul of the World

Mighty Hekate, Soul of the World,
Let me see myself in Your reflection,
Awaken in me Your fire of creation,
Reveal in me faith, love and truth.

Mighty Hekate, Soul of the World,
Within Your fiery rays, I am reborn,
The sacred spark of my soul rekindled,
Through Your flames I become as limitless as Your eternal light.

Mighty Hekate, Soul of the World,
Like Your serpent, I am an agent of creation.
Upon Your horse, I ride confidently through this life.
As the fierce hound, I am the protector.

Mighty Hekate, Soul of the World,
May You be woven into my very being.
Your colors of black, white and red
Becoming my essential fire.

Mighty Hekate, Soul of the World,
Your black threads ensoul my emotions, turning them towards love.
While the white strands weave truth into my intellect,
And the red sews the strength of faith into all my actions.

Mighty Hekate, Soul of the World,

May Your weapons of power become mine.
Piercing the veil of hatred with Your fire-forged sword,
Your strength a burning shield protecting me from harm.

Hekate, Soul of the World,
May I use Your weapons as a light upon the world.
I gladly receive the key of Your infinite wisdom,
May I use it well.

Hail Hekate, Guardian.
Hail Hekate, Guide.
Hail Hekate, Gatekeeper.
Hail Hekate, Soul of the World.

Hekate's Rocks and Minerals

We can use rocks and mineral in the Three Key Colors, especially when they also reflect the energetic properties associated with each of Hekate's Three Keys. While there are many different rocks and mineral that can fit into this structure, I am going to focus on clear/white quartz, red jasper and black obsidian. In addition, Hekate in the ancient texts and contemporary writings has been associated with other stones, including pearl, iron, bronze, gold, silver, and moonstone. Working with rocks and minerals is like the techniques used for the other correspondences. We can call upon their energetic properties to assist us when we are petitioning Hekate for her attention and to add to our magical workings. Magical stones should be prepared using the techniques of cleansing and consecrating discussed previously. For example, you can place new ones on a windowsill or outside for a lunar cycle to cleanse them of nonessential energies.

Once your clear/white quartz, red jasper and black obsidian are ready for use, you can place them on your salt strophalos and then pass them through incense (using a blend of our three Key Herbs) while asking Hekate to bless them. The association of Hekate with jasper and obsidian dates to the ancient use of magical coins. There are several examples of these coins made from these minerals. Place at least one of each of the three on your main altar, with extra on hand for specific workings. The easiest way to work with stones is by carrying them with you after infusing them with your intent. You can keep them in your bag, pockets, or even inside your bra (I do this often!). Infusing a stone with an intention can be accomplished by holding it in your hand during a working and concentrating on connecting your desire with the energetic properties of the rock. You can also, or in addition (that's what I usually do), pass it back and forth across the incense you are burning during a working. Like with bay laurel leaves, you can write your intention directly on the stone. This creates a magical coin like the ones from antiquity and is a very powerful talisman.

Black Obsidian

There are other black stones suited for representing Hekate as Guardian in her Under World aspect, such as hematite and iron. I've chosen black obsidian since it was commonly used by the ancients in their magical coins featuring Hekate. The unique aspects of obsidian render it highly reflective of Under World energy because it is born out of the fire of the Under World since it is a volcanic stone. Obsidian offers a unique structure that is different than most other minerals. The structure of obsidian is rather unique for it resembles glass rather than a typical rock. This renders obsidian both incredibly durable and able to be rather easily broken into fragments. The ancients across many cultures used the fragments they would break off a large chunk of obsidian to fashion tools and weapons.

Obsidian is a natural receptacle and conduit for use in magic. We can deposit unwanted energies into a hunk of it. As a conduit, we can work with obsidian's energies to both connect to the Under World and the earth, and to release ourselves from these connections. Work with obsidian when you are focusing on your lower self, for emotional healing and to help connect with Hekate as Guardian. If you are struggling with anxiety, depression or fear, visualize your distress being accepted into obsidian. This stone will readily accept these emotions. Obsidian can be carried for protection. A final way to use obsidian is for grounding when you are feeling disconnected or at the beginning of a working. Holding the stone in your left hand (since it is of the Under World), envision its energy coursing through you connecting yourself to the earth beneath your feet. If you are feeling too chthonic ("of the earth"), use obsidian to lessen this connection. Use obsidian in connection with sage and Cups in the Tarot.

Red Jasper

Red jasper is the stone of the Middle World because of its properties of banishing, encouragement and well-being. It is there to help us along our life's journey and can be worked with as a symbol of Hekate as Guide. To evoke the properties of red jasper, hold it between both hands at your heart center. As a banishing stone, you can write the thing that you need to be freed from on it, pass it through incense smoke and then bury it off your property. I have thrown banishing jasper into the ocean. As a stone of encouragement and well-being, it is unsurpassed. My oldest son went through a very difficult adolescence. As part of helping him heal, I was directed to red jasper by my witchy mentor. After he began keeping it with him constantly, he started to improve. I should write that it was after he started to believe that he could heal, and that the jasper would help him. Belief is so powerful when working with correspondences. If our energy isn't aligned with the properties of any correspondence, its efficacy will be greatly diminished. If you need encouragement, hold the jasper at your heart center while repeating affirmations. Then wear it next to your skin. To enhance general well-being, wear it in the same way. You can place one by the entrance to your home for the benefit of all who live there and the physical structure.

Clear/White Quartz

I am using both clear and white quartz because the former usually must be purchased, but the latter can often be found in gravel and our natural environment. Where I live on the Atlantic coast of Nova Scotia, white quartz can easily be found on the shore. The energy of the two is the same. Quartz unlike obsidian and red jasper is not associated with Hekate in antiquity. Perhaps this is because it wasn't available. However, clear quartz is seen as the most useful mineral available for magical purposes by contemporary practitioners. Quartz is available in many different forms, with each type having distinct energetic properties. As such, it is important that you work with either the clear or the white form as a correspondence of Hekate as Gatekeeper.

I recommend purchasing a clear crystal point for placing on your main altar. You can use it as a wand to focus your energy during workings. This is one of the three ways that we will be working with quartz – to help us focus. In addition, we can use clear quartz to draw our energy up to our higher self and the astral realm of the Third World. Consider purchasing a piece to use exclusively this way. Envision the quartz as a gateway to the realm of Hekate as Gatekeeper, where you can gain knowledge of her mysteries and she will share her wisdom with you. In workings, clear or white quartz can be used as an all-purpose correspondence that will boost the energies of the herbs, other stones, colors, etc. that you're using.

A final note about rocks and minerals is that I urge you to purchase them in as ethical a way as possible. Many of the mines where these treasures come from use harsh labor practices. This is why I try to find the stones in their natural settings. If you wish to do this, you can feel free to substitute white, red and black rocks that you find in your surroundings. Otherwise, do your research and buy from reputable dealers.

Exercise: Correspondence Quest

Going on a quest to find a magical object – in this case correspondences – is a fun technique for determining which one is right for you. Sometimes objects spontaneously appear. The best personal story I have of this is the time that I was out for a run in an urban neighborhood when I practically tripped over a fist-sized chunk of black obsidian in the middle of the sidewalk. You've developed your observation skills to the point now that correspondences that you need to be working with may be spontaneously presenting themselves to you in a similar manner. However, we can also go on a journey to find the right ones. This quest can be a metaphysical journey, an actual adventure or both. Our focus is on doing an actual quest, but I've added some ways to do a metaphysical version at the end of this section. I love going on an adventure quest to find new correspondences. I am my most alive when I am in wild places. Going in search of correspondences outdoors is a fantastic form of witchery! As with any magical undertaking, begin by setting an intention prior to embarking on your quest.

Writing the Correspondence Quest Intention

What is it you'd like to find?
- Will you be content with whatever is presented to you or do you want something specific?

How will you be using this correspondence?
- Perhaps you're hoping to find items for your altar or in-gredients for a working. If you're after a general use sort of correspondence, that's perfectly acceptable. Just make

sure you include this in your intention.

How would you like it to be presented to you?
- Often, I add to an intention designed to help me find a new correspondence something like, "bring my attention to that which I am sure to find" so the probability of missing the object is reduced.

Here's an example: "Mighty Hekate, Queen, I call upon you and your energies to reveal to me that which I seek while I am on my quest at _____ to help me with my _____ for use _____ on this day _____." You get the idea. The more specific, the better. When I created the witch jar that brought us our little cottage on the coast, everything on my list was included. However, I wrote "fireplace" but did not specify that it had to be in working condition. I have a beautiful fireplace, but no chimney!

Once your intention is set, record it in your Book of Shadows with the date, lunar phase and astrological information. In general, this is a good way to record all entries. Of course, it's important to consider all these variables before doing any working, but setting an intention is just the first part of a spell. The important thing is to now choose the optimal time for doing the working, in this case it is your correspondence quest. There are a few other factors to consider in planning your adventure:

Planning Your Correspondence Quest

Planetary and lunar considerations
- In general, you want to attract the object to you, so the waxing moon phase is problematic. If you must do your question during this period, transmute the energy by adding something like this to your intention, "by the power of the waxing moon, all barriers will be removed."

- It's a good idea to also consult with the dominant planetary energies for the day of your planned outing. I use a wall calendar that contains all this information. If the planets seem wonky on your chosen day, add a bit to your intention to transmute their energy.

Location

- The more remote, the better the location is for receiving an object. Although it's possible to have a correspondence come forward to you in a more urban environment, there's a lot of nonessential and unnatural energies swirling about.
- Revisit special places. I used to go to this large urban park a few times a week. I used to wander down the less traveled trails, searching for cool places for rituals. One day I found such a place. It even had a bench and a dining-room table sized rock. If you don't have a spot like this, maybe your first quest is to find it!
- Research the parks and nature reserves in your area if you don't have a location already selected. Get outside! The best witchery is always done in nature.

The Quest Begins

- Copy your intention from your Book of Shadows onto a piece of paper that you can carry with you. Don't forget a backpack and plastic bags to carry home your correspondence(s).
- When you arrive at the location, read the intention out loud.
- Pay attention to your surroundings. Notice the plants, any wildlife and the built environment. A witch is an observer of all things because we know that signs are there waiting for us to discover them.
- The object will be something unusual, such as the hunk of

black obsidian I found or an unexpected animal sighting. I've had so many of these! Land-locked ducks in the middle of a blizzard, snakes in my urban driveway and in the pool, a lone feather on the shore. If it's an animal sighting, then you won't have anything to carry home with you except the creature's energy.

- When you find your object, ask it if it is yours. The energy from it will be your answer.
- The object will not be something that is harmful to remove from a site.

After the Quest

- Cleanse the object only if it feels necessary.
- Sit with your object. Hold it in your hands, study it. Get to know each other.
- Research the standard applications of your object but use it how it feels right to you.
- Record the information about the object in your Book of Shadows, including the lunar phase and planetary considerations. You may want to develop your own correspondence database with this information in it.
- Continue to build your relationship with the object in the way that feels right to you. You can keep it on your altar, sleep with it beside you or carry it next to your skin.

Metaphysical Correspondence Quest

If it's not possible to go on an actual adventure, you can have your correspondence(s) revealed to you in the Other World using various techniques such as a journey, fire scrying or ask Hekate to send you a message:

- You can adapt the World Soul Journey so that it becomes a quest for your correspondence(s).
- Use the fire scrying technique with the intention of the

flames revealing your object.

- Refer to the recommendations in the lesson on your relationship with Hekate for ways to contact her regarding your desired object.

Summary

Correspondences are things that we use to connect with Hekate and for use on their own or in combination with others for magical workings. Some common correspondences include animals, colors and stones. There are several different animals associated with Hekate throughout history. The three most powerfully connected to her are dogs, horses and snakes. Although there are many colors that can be associated with Hekate, black, red and white are the three most important. The rocks and minerals that we work with can also be these colors if their energetic properties correspond to the appropriate aspects. Black obsidian is symbolic of the Under World and Hekate as Guardian, while clear or white quartz can connect us to the Upper World and Hekate as Gatekeeper. Finally, red jasper is a powerful ally for our Middle World journey. Going on a correspondence quest will be an adventure that brings magical objects to you.

Lesson 10: Hekate's Garden

There are so many plants associated with Hekate in her three millennia of history. Some are directly sourced from the ancient texts. The most extensive list of plants associated with her is found in this description of Hekate's Garden in this fourth-century CE version of the tale of Jason and the Argonauts:[41]

In the innermost recess of the enclosure was a sacred grove, shaded by green trees. Therein were many laurels, cornels, tall shoots, and grass, within which grew short plants with powerful roots: asphodel, beautiful maidenhair, rushes, galingale, delicate verbena, sage, hedge-mustard, purple honeysuckle, healing cassidony, flourishing field basil, mandrake, hulwort; in addition fluffy dittany, fragrant saffron, nose-smart; and also lion-foot, greenbrier, camomile, black poppy, alcua, all-heal, white hellebore, aconite, and other noxious plants which are born from the earth. In the middle, the trunk of a great oak reached high, and the tree's branches overspread the grove.

Plants associated with Hekate beyond this list include almond, basil, chamomile, dandelion, frankincense, garlic, lavender and rose. There are many more that can be connected to her various aspects because of common energetic properties, such as mugwort. As an herbalist, I use a lot of plant energy in my workings and in healing. I have selected three herbs from Her Garden that we can use to represent Hekate's Three Roles. Exploring herbs is a fantastic witchy thing to do, and I enthusiastically encourage you to learn about the plants in Hekate's Garden and beyond. The plants in Hekate's Garden that I have been able to connect directly to Her through my research are listed below. Some of the items are contemporary but with traditional connections. I consulted ancient texts, herbals throughout the Middle Ages until the twentieth century

and reviewed contemporary associations. If I couldn't verify
the connection to Hekate in the historical records, I excluded
the modern plants. I've added botanical "cousins" for some of
the ancient or rare plants. These plants share similar energetic
properties and uses but are more accessible to us. I've added
the energetic realm most appropriate for working with each
botanical. However, in most cases the realm is subjective, and
you can use it in the way that best suits your goal. I added a few
uses for each herb, but there are many other applications of each
one that I haven't mentioned. I encourage you to explore the list
and study the ones that you feel drawn to.

Plants in Hekate's Garden

Plant	Uses
Aconite	Banishing; flying ointments; poison
Almond	Offerings; love magic; sacred fires
Asphodel	Death work; communicating with Hekate
Basil	Connecting to dragon energy; courage; initiation
Bay Laurel	Attraction; manifestation; psychic development
Belladonna	Banishing; poison; "war" workings
Betony	Calming; protection; reversal magic
Benzoin	Personal development; visions
Bittersweet	Protection; secrets; revelations
Cardamom	Passion; sex
Dandelion	Healing; tonic
Datura	Poison; reversal magic
Devil's Trumpet	Poison; witchcraft
Dittany	Death work; teaching
Frankincense	Devotional incense; focus; self-discipline
Galingale	Lust; money; success
Garlic	Invoking; offerings; protection
Ginger	Health; protection; purification

Honeysuckle	Metaphysical awareness; travelling to the Realms
Lavender	Calming; working with serpent energy
Licorice Root	Communication; writing
Mandrake	Clairvoyance; creativity
Moonwort	Angels; divination
Morning Glory	Affection; family
Mugwort	Psychic development; witchcraft
Mustard	Growth; prosperity; growth
Myrrh	Boosts any magical experience; offerings
Nightshade	Poison; removal of toxic people
Oak	Loyalty; offerings
Olive	Base for potions and oils; offerings
Rose	Balance; love; secrecy; offerings
Saffron	Calm; desire; fertility
Sage	Purification; protection; rituals
Storax	Communication; devotional incense
Verbena	Cleansing; creativity
Watercress	Psychic development; visions
Willow	Communication; death work
Wormwood	Banishing; healing; personal development work
Yew	Strength; witchcraft

Practice: Keeping Your Own Hekate's Garden Record

There may be plants that you already have a connection with, and you can certainly include them in your Hekate's Garden. It may be an herb that you feel strongly aligned with or a favorite flower. Research this plant. Discover its properties, uses and correspondences using a reference manual. See if you can connect this plant's details to Hekate, either directly or through mutual correspondences. Record this plant as the first entry in Hekate's Garden in your Book of Shadows. In general, you should keep detailed information about the plants you feel most connected to in this section of your Book of Shadows. Like with the other correspondences, the ones with known associations to Hekate are happy to share space with ones that have the most meaning to you.

Using Hekate's Garden

The above list will get you started working with plants that are associated with Hekate. Parts of the plant you can work with usually include leaves, roots, seeds and fruit pits. The parts of some plants have different energetic properties. For example, a root can be used one way, but the flower another. Dandelion flowers can be used for manifestation, while the root is good for developing tenacity and Under World energy. Oak branches make excellent wands, while the leaves and acorns are excellent as offerings and the bark can be used for a general tonic.

The plants that we'll be focusing on reflect the Three Roles of Hekate:

- Sage is used as a correspondence of Hekate as Guardian.
- Bay laurel is the correspondence for Hekate as Guide.
- Hekate as Gatekeeper is associated with mugwort.

These are three fascinating herbs with multiple uses and well-established connections to Hekate and witchcraft.

General Plant Use Tips

Carefully research each botanical that you're considering using and then decide what makes sense to you. Be mindful of handling dangerous plants and careful when burning things. Plants can be naturally harvested or purchased. Depending on where you live, you can find one or more of our key plants growing naturally in your area or you can cultivate them yourself. All three of the plants grow well in most climates, although in the cooler ones the plants will have to winter indoors. I always bless and cleanse the purchased dried plants when they are first brought into my home. That way they are ready to be used. I keep my dried magical plants in the kitchen but separate from regular cooking herbs. Some can be used for both purposes. I encourage you to add to this list of three any that make sense to you. Harvesting plants is a fantastic way to enliven your witchcraft. You can learn about the natural flora in your area, or you can grow your own plants. Growing challenging plants associated with Hekate, like mandrake, can be a very rewarding experience. For local harvesting, there can be indigenous plants in your area or cultivated ones.

Herbal Magic

I enjoy reading the ancients' approach to witchcraft because the approach is very different than our modern harm-reduction approach (for most of us). The ancient witches were heavy into poisonous concoctions, binding and destroying their enemies. For example, Circe was so furious when Glaucus chose Scylla over her, she transformed the maiden into a sea monster invoking Hecate in her poisonous blend of herbs:

> She made a brew of herbs, and as she cooked them
> She sang aloud songs learned from Hecate –
> Singing that should make any mortal tremble.[42]

I absolutely love this quote because it is exactly what I typically do with herbs. I love witchin' in the kitchen, cooking up a potion to use in a spell. I'm going to talk about spell construction later. For now, let's explore the various ways that plants can be used as correspondences.

All the parts of a plant can be used for magical purposes, including the entire plant, the branches and trunk, bark, leaves, seeds, flowers, fruit, resins (the gummy stuff on some plants) and roots. For the three botanicals we're focusing on, the typical use is of the leaves and stems. However, if you have a bay laurel tree, you can certainly work with the branches. You can fashion them into a wand or burn them in a magical fire. In addition, the parts of the plant can be transformed into essential oil or magical water. For example, frankincense is a resin that we can use in its natural state as part of incense or we can work with it as an essential oil. I am a big fan of making and using different types of magical waters for use on their own and in potions. Rosewater made from the wild ones that grow on my property are a staple in my magic. Magical water is easy to make. The three herbs I chose for this course can all be made into magical water on their own or in combination. The easiest form of magical water to make involves using about a cup of purified water and a teaspoon or so of each herb. Combine in a magically prepared bottle. Say a blessing over it while you seal it. Place on the window ledge where it will be exposed to the sun and moon. Leave it there for one full lunar cycle. If you can leave it outside, that's even better.

Magical Water

Magical water is one way that herbs can be used. Once you've got your magic water you can blend it with other ingredients (e.g., coins, hair, and correspondences to create a potion). An even simpler technique is just to use the herb in its natural state. To use their natural state during a working, you can hold them in your hand or place them on your altar. The three herbs we're using are all safe to touch. However, there are many herbs associated with Hekate (e.g., belladonna, aconite) that must be handled with gloves because of their poisonous nature. To prepare an herb for use in its natural state, simply rub it between your palms to activate the natural properties, after it's been cleansed of unnecessary energies. You can also use a mortar and pestle made from a semi-porous stone (e.g., granite) to release the energies. A mortar and pestle are very useful when you are combining herbs, making a large amount, or using herbs that shouldn't be handled.

Botanical Containment

Placing herbs in a prepared bag or box is a technique used to harness their properties over an extended time. You can also place them in a magical container on your window ledge for a lunar cycle to infuse them with the energy of the moon, combining two correspondences. It's easy to make a small bag for holding your herbs. Take a square of fabric that's been prepared along with string. Place the herbs in the middle, then gather the fabric together until you can easily wrap the string around it.

Burning Botanicals

Although herbs prepared this way are powerful allies in our magic, there are additional benefits in burning them for most workings. If it's not possible for you to burn herbs, you can create the same energy by putting them in a low (about 200 degrees) oven for a few minutes. Warming them this way releases their energies in a different way than holding them. If you are going to be burning herbs as incense, a heat-proof dish (i.e. a censor) and small charcoal discs are necessary. These are easily found online.

Using Larger Botanical Pieces

Working with larger parts of a plant, such as branches and leaves is another form of botanical magic. You can make a wand out of a branch of a bay laurel tree, for example. You can also grow plants like mugwort and sage as part of your devotional practice. All three can be directly thrown into a fire to give the flames extra magic. There are so many ways of working with herbs, including the three that we're focusing on.

Hekate's Key Herbs

The plants in Hekate's garden are many and bountiful. Three

herbs that are strongly associated with her from antiquity to the present day are bay laurel, mugwort and sage. All three have many diverse purposes but are accessible to beginners especially regarding their connections to each of the three energetic realms. Each of these herbs can be worked with on their own. I've chosen three properties of each one, although there are many other uses for them. In addition, each of the Key Herbs can be used in a general way to strengthen any magical working. All three are also powerful for purification of the body and ritual space.

Bay Laurel

Bay leaves are a common kitchen witch ingredient in spells. This humble herb – probably in your cupboard – has been associated with Hekate since ancient times.[43] The use of bay has become quite common in contemporary witchcraft, with many a simple spell proclaiming that money can be manifested through burning a single leaf or carrying one in your wallet. Bay laurel is associated with Air and Fire, so it is perfectly suited for working with Hekate as Guide of our Middle World journey, as it represents the combination of the Upper World energy of Air and the Under World energy of Fire. For this book, we are working with Bay Laurel as a correspondence of Hekate as Guide, her Middle World role as guide through our life's journey. While the properties of bay laurel are many, and I thoroughly encourage you to learn more about multiple magical uses of this fascinating tree, for our purposes, our focus is on using it in three different ways:

- **Banishing**: removal of toxic people, ill will, negative energy, etc.
- **Manifestation**: Bay laurel is an all-purpose tool for manifesting prosperity, especially good for finances and creating opportunities.
- **Motivation**: use bay laurel to help get yourself going and to help increase your magical energy.

Bay laurel can be used in a variety of rituals and spells. I often use it to purify the space and myself prior to calling upon Hekate in any magical working. Bay laurel lights easily, so the use of a charcoal disc can be considered optional. It will also help ignite other herbs when used in a blend or incense. It's simple to recreate one of the ancient incenses using grain, bay laurel and wheat bran.

There are two basic ways to use Bay laurel in conjunction with Hekate: by burning it or by infusing it with your intention. If you are burning it, make sure that you have it in a heat-proof dish and watch the flames. It can be quite sparky. Use the smoke to symbolically release the intention into the world and then bury the ash from the leaf. To infuse it with your intention, you can write on the leaf using a one-word representation of your desired outcome or design a sigil for the leaf. Depending on your desired outcome, you can either bury it or carry it with you. Burying the leaf is indicated when you wish to remove something, while carrying it is appropriate for attracting something or for general protection. I have a special fondness for bay laurel for an additional reason beyond its accessibility, multiple uses and association with Hekate – it's associated with Gemini which happens to be my sun sign and with one of my companion deities, Mercury.

Mugwort

Mugwort, a type of wormwood, has magical and medicinal uses dating back as long as Hekate's known history. As wormwood, it is often cited as an ingredient in the spells of *The Greek Magical Papyri*. The deities associated with the herb are many, but in contemporary witchcraft, Artemis is most often cited as a goddess connected to mugwort. This stems from the Latin name of the plant, artemisia vulgaris, which some interpret to be associated with Artemis. However, the plant is named after an ancient Greek queen rather than the goddess. This ancient

Artemesia was a sort of revolutionary healer, and it is this origin that reflects mugwort's powerful restorative powers. Mugwort has long been associated with the feminine divine, including Venus in addition to Artemis, as it is very useful as an aid with reproductive issues. Mugwort is an herb of the moon, indicating that we can use it to connect with Hekate as Gatekeeper, her Upper World side. Mugwort is associated with Air and Earth, representing our connection to the Upper World as residents of the Middle World. In addition, mugwort is often used to enhance psychic abilities, providing us with energy for working with Hekate's mysteries. Mugwort is the Upper World herb that we are working with for the remainder of this book. Here are the three properties that we'll be exploring:

- **Healing**: mugwort is a powerful agent for personal development work, letting go of the past and restoration of happiness.
- **Psychic development**: enhances all our visionary skills, as a conduit to the dream world, and for sharpening our divination work.
- **Receiving:** great for acquisition magic and attracting things to ourselves.

Mugwort can be used in ways that reflect these three energetic themes. For dream work, you can make a sachet out of the herb and sleep with it under your pillow. To enhance divination using the Tarot, prime the cards for use by passing them through mugwort smoke nine times. For personal healing, make a magical water using mugwort and anoint yourself with it in the morning and evening. You can also purchase mugwort essential oil to make this even more powerful. For acquisition magic, hold mugwort and state your intention. Then place the mugwort into a prepared bag and carry it with you.

Sage

Smudging with sage has become commonplace for many modern-day practitioners. This act is often associated with Northern American First Nations peoples, but the magical uses of sage were reported by the ancient Greek writers. In fact, sage is listed as one of the plants in the description of Hekate's Garden in the *Orphic Argonautica*. Using sage as part of a purification and protection process at the beginning of a rite reflects the role of Hekate as Guardian and Under World energy.

- **Insight**: Sage is great for when we are trying to understand our own internal processes, thoughts, emotions and actions.
- **Projecting**: very useful when we want to send energy out into the universe, for when we want to stand up for ourselves, or for using the energy of creation.
- **Protection**: defense against harm of all sorts, including psychic attack and curses.

Use sage with the techniques I've described for bay laurel and mugwort. You can write your intention on a ribbon, tie it to a piece of sage and then burn them both in a heat-safe container. For gaining insight to your own inner workings, make a sachet and wear it on your body while contemplating these things. You can keep a dish of sage in your personal space to help bring more clarity in a similar fashion. For protection, it is most helpful when burnt while listing the forces that you need to be shielded from. You can call upon Hekate as protector while burning sage.

Exercise: Making the Three Keys Incense

The Three Keys Incense is an all-purpose blend of bay laurel, mugwort and sage. You'll be using this for many purposes, from part of your ritual of devotion to use in spellwork.

Requirements

- At least one ounce each of bay laurel, mugwort and sage
- Three candles – black, red and white
- Three small containers with lids – black, red and white
- Mortar and pestle
- A small piece each of black obsidian, red jasper and clear/white quartz
- Larger container with lid for storing the prepared incense
- For burning: charcoal disks and heat-proof dish
- For making magical water: purified water and bottle

Preparation

If possible, you should always use plants that are harvested ethically and are organic. I purchase herbs in bulk because I use them for magical and personal use. If you're new to herbalism, I suggest ordering a few ounces of each one. You will also need three candles and three small containers for the herbs. The colors associated with the herbs are: black for sage, red for bay laurel and white for mugwort. If you can't get candles and jars in the appropriate colors, you can use a marker or paint the matching hue on white or clear things.

Preparing the Candles

Candles should be dressed prior to their first use; you can do this by keeping them on your Salt Strophalos for a few days. Prior to taking them out, make sure you rub them with the salt all over. You'll need three small pieces of black obsidian, red jasper and clear or white quartz as well, so put them on the Salt Strophalos if they aren't yet prepared. Same for the three herbs. Say a few words seeking Hekate's blessing over their use when you're ready to take them off the salt.

You'll also need a mortar and pestle for blending. You can use a prepared bowl and spoon instead. The final thing required is a container with a lid for storing the completed incense. You can decorate this container using the three colors and other things if you wish.

The preparation should be done on the Full Moon if possible.

Making the Incense

As with any magical working, you should purify yourself and the space in which you'll be doing the activity. Once you and the space are ready, arrange the three candles, containers, stones and the larger container near a representation of Hekate and your Salt Strophalos. The colors should be arranged as black, red and white in that order. If you are going to be burning the incense immediately after, have the tools you'll need ready in this space. Same goes for making magical water.

Begin by reciting something like: *Hail Hekate, Mighty Queen of All, Creatrix and World Soul, Bless the creation of this incense and its use.*

Light the black candle, saying: *Hail Hekate as Guardian, Goddess of the Under World, bless this working.* Place the sage in the container, *Bless this sage.* Place the obsidian on top of the herb, *Obsidian. mine, your energy with the sage is now combined.*

Light the red candle: *Hail Hekate as Guide, Goddess of the Middle World, bless this working.* Place the bay laurel in the appropriate container, *Bless this bay laurel.* Place the red jasper on top, *Red jasper lend your energy to the bay, combing to make magic come my way.*

Light the white candle: *Hail Hekate as Gatekeeper, Goddess of the Upper World, bless this working.* Say "*bless this mugwort*" as you put it in the right container. Place the quartz in the corresponding container, saying "*Mugwort strengthened more by this quartz, I implore.*"

Pour the stones and the herbs into your blending vessel, whether it's mortar and pestle or a bowl and spoon. Mix the herbs in a clockwise direction three times and then counter clockwise three times. Then pat down on them to gently release some of their properties so they can combine their energies. Do this in a series of threes. Repeat this process three times. While doing this you can chant, *Bay, sage, mugwort. Herbs I command with my own hands through Hekate's help, their magic is mine.*

Once you've finished, place the blend in the large container. Thank Hekate for her blessing over the incense. You'll feel her energy depart as you extinguish the candles. Now you can practice burning them or make a magical water.

Summary

Hekate's Garden contains many plants that can be used for devotional and magical purposes. Preparation and use of plants in witchcraft is a fascinating part of rituals and spells. Bay laurel, mugwort and sage are three herbs that have powerful connections to Hekate. We can use them in various ways to enhance our rites. We can combine them into an all-purpose incense that can be used during devotional workings, they can be made into magical water and used to enhance other plants. Starting your own record of the botanicals that you work with in Hekate's Garden is a great activity that will heighten your knowledge of herbalism.

Lesson 11: Divination

We look to divination when we are seeking answers to life's questions. As devotees of Hekate, we turn to her for guidance and advice. Until this point in the course, we've explored direct messages from Hekate. In the next lesson, on sacred space we explore the realm of the Other World through intentional lucid dreaming. In this one, we're focusing on using the Tarot in connection with Hekate's energy. Whatever means of divination we're using, the answers we're after usually concern trying to find out what is going to happen in the future. Often, we have a choice to make and we want assurance that we are selecting the right path. However, divination is most useful when we are looking for insight into our own feelings, thoughts and actions. Divination reflects our energies. Sometimes, we need clarification. Other times, we have forgotten what we already know.

The way we approach divination is greatly influenced by our personal beliefs about our capabilities and how we see the divine and metaphysical forces. I am not going to tell you which approach is best for using divination. My personal experience is that predicting the future is a complicated business when using divinatory tools, like the Tarot. I prefer using them for guidance and insight. Hekate's direct messages are always on point, but She rarely tells me the future.

Understanding: Exploring Divination

What does divination mean to you? Is it a tool for predicting the future, personal development or both? What are your favorite divination tools? Explore your thoughts about divination in your journal.

The Tarot

Tarot cards can be used in two basic ways: using their symbolic imagery in workings as correspondences and for divination. As correspondences, we can use the standard meaning of a card as a source of energy. For example, the Tower is a card of transformation. If we are doing a working with the intention of manifesting great change, we might choose the Tower if we want to really shake things up.

Preparing Cards for Use

If you don't already have a basic understanding of Tarot, then I suggest you do a bit of research so that you are better informed about the cards. If you are going to be using a new deck, ensure that it is properly cleansed before delving in. While there are many ways to do this, I typically take a new deck and put it in a black bag for a while before cleansing it even. Then I will put it in the Salt Strophalos for a while. Then I will do a consecration ritual where I ask for Hekate's blessing over the cards while I pass the deck back and forth over incense smoke. If the deck is for my personal use, I'll carry it with me in my bag and put it under my pillow at night until I feel the cards are in tune with my vibration. Those are just a few tips to get your deck ready for use.

Tarot Cards as Correspondences

Through the matching of Hekatean energy with the suits of the Tarot, the elements and the astrological signs can also be added as correspondences. Hekate as Guardian is reflected in the Cups, with the element of water and the west. Associated astrological signs are Pisces, Cancer and Scorpio. Pentacles is the suit of Hekate as Guide, corresponding with the element of earth (north). Capricorn, Taurus and Virgo are situated in the element of earth. Air and the east are linked to Swords and to Hekate as Gatekeeper, with Aquarius, Gemini and Libra as the signs. Fire is used to represent the fiery energy of creation and destruction of Hekate as the World Soul, so it's associated with Wands (fire/south). Signs associated as Aries, Sagittarius and Leo. I've often used specific Tarot cards as part of a working, using a specific card to reinforce the overall energy of a spell, as a representation of Hekate in a ritual or as a focal point for personal development.

Using Tarot's Imagery

In the classic Rider-Waite Tarot deck, snakes are featured in four different cards: The Magician, the Lovers, the Wheel of Fortune and the Seven of Cups. Wolves, a sort of canine, are often depicted in the Moon card, while horses are featured usually with the Chariot and sometimes the Princes are on them. These are examples of how we can combine correspondences, in this case Hekate's Serpents and the Tarot. We can use the meaning of a card with the associated Hekatean energy to add strength to our workings. There are many other individual cards that we can associate with Hekate, Her Keys and her various epithets.

Three of the suits can be directly linked to Hekate's Roles: Cups is representative of Hekate as Guardian, Pentacles is associated with the Middle World of Hekate as Guide and Swords, the suit of Air, is symbolic of Hekate as Gatekeeper. The fourth suit, Wands, as its fiery nature is well-suited to Hekate as the World Soul. The Minor and Major Arcana cards can be associated with each Hekate in many ways. I've already mentioned the Moon for its association with dogs, but this card can also be used as symbolic of Hekate as Guardian with the imagery of the moon.

Exercise: Hekate and the Major Arcana

In this exercise, you are going to construct a table for situating the cards of the Major Arcana within each of the four vectors (Guide, Guardian, Gatekeeper and World Soul) as best as possible. Some of the cards of the Major Arcana are easily to position, but others have complex meanings. You may decide to include one aspect of a card within one of Hekate's roles and a different meaning of the same card in another. The structure of the exercise is very simple, but the task itself is quite challenging because it requires you to apply your knowledge of Hekate to a complex system. This is an excellent way to develop your skills in using correspondences in conjunction with Hekate. You can use a word web to help you organize each of the specific "sides" of Hekate with the various cards using what you know about Hekate and your own intuitive reading of each of the Major Arcana cards. When you've finished with your intuitive analysis, refer to the standardized one for the deck you are using.

Exercise: Establishing a Daily Tarot Practice

A daily two-card Tarot practice exploring approach and avoidance can be used to receive Hekate's guidance and to help us learn the energy of the cards. The ways we practice approach and avoidance across a variety of situations are indicators of personal well-being. For example, using avoidance coping can be hurtful except when it's a problem that we can't solve. In contrast, approaching things that we don't have much control over can be disastrous. Coping is a mixture of both approach and avoidance. Balance is found in knowing whether to approach or avoid an event, person or situation. We are continually engaging in approach/avoidance thoughts and behaviors without giving much thought to the underlying concept.

Approach/Avoidance in Magic

The ubiquity of the approach/avoidance duality is also found in magic. Probably the most common application is working with the different phases of the lunar cycle. I can use the energy of the waning moon to help with spells of avoidance. These are the things that I want to remove from my life. The opposite energy comes with the waxing moon – that energy is for things that I want closer to me. This is approach energy. Full Moon energy is a balance of both approach and avoidance energy. The Dark Moon can be interpreted as the absence of both.

There are so many ways that approach/avoidance can be used for interpreting the Tarot. I'm going to use a few examples to illustrate some of the different ways that approach and avoidance can apply to the cards. For this discussion, I'm using the traditional Tarot deck, with the four suits of Cups (Water), Pentacles (Earth), Swords (Air), and Wands (Fire) and the Minor/Major Arcana framework since this is the one most of us know.

Doing the Reading

I suggest doing the daily spread first thing in the morning or at bedtime in preparation for the following day. There are so many ways to pull two cards that I'll leave it up to you. The important thing is to concentrate on approach or avoidance as you shuffle your cards and then pull one at a time. I generally shuffle once, then hold my intention while I shuffle again, pull that card and repeat the process for the second card. If you're using an app, concentrate on either "approach" or "avoidance" before you select a card. Once you have your two cards, contemplate the meaning of the card in terms of approach or avoidance before looking up the standard definition. Drawing the cards is simple, interpreting may not always be! I hope the few examples I provided help with thinking about the cards in terms of approach and avoidance.

Summary

Divination can be used to peer into the future or for personal development work. While there are many divinatory tools available, the Tarot is especially useful in Modern Hekatean Witchcraft because the cards can be easily identified with characteristics and roles of Hekate. The Tarot can be used as a correspondence in workings, as a reflection of various aspects

of Hekate and for divination. The Hekate Approach-Avoidance
Tarot practice reveals Hekate's wisdom to use through what we
should approach and avoid.

Lesson 12: Types of Sacred Space

When it comes to sacred spaces, there are two broad categories: naturally sacred spaces and those we manufacture. Natural sacred spaces associated with Hekate are the three worlds and liminal areas. When we manufacture a sacred space, we are attempting to create – and work with – Hekate's energy. This can be accomplished by establishing altars and shrines and through casting of energetic spaces. We can also travel to a type of sacred space, the dream world.

Land, Sea and Sky

Consider that the entire planet is sacred to Hekate. In the ancient texts, she was assigned dominion over the three parts of the earth – land, sea and sky – by Zeus.[44] As the World Soul, Hekate's three sides merge synergistically to fuel all living things. The Realm associated with Hekate as the World Soul is the Liminal Realm, that will be discussed later. We can use the three parts of the world as correspondences to help us connect to Hekate and with our workings.

Using this framework, we can choose representations of the three parts of the world to include on our altars and in our workings. In addition, we can use physical locations that reflect the juncture of land, sea and sky as powerful locations for rites. This is a type of energetic crossroads, a liminal space where all three parts come together.

Liminal Spaces

As key bearer, Hekate stands between worlds and at thresholds solidifying boundaries. In many of the ancient tales, she plays the role of the mediator, neither leaving us to our own devices nor telling us what to do. She is the Queen of the In-Between. The most sacred locations to Hekate are those spaces in between, such as places where land, sea and sky meet. This is one example of the type of liminal space most honored in Modern Hekatean Witchcraft: the three-way crossroads. This understanding of the special role of the three-way crossroads for devotees of Hekate extends back to ancient practices.[45] The Liminal Realm is the energetic world where Hekate abides. It is at the nexus of the three other realms. As humans, we experience the fourth realm as the Other World, the land of dreams and other metaphysical experiences outside of the four other realms.

Liminal Times

There are liminal times of the day as well, including dawn and twilight when I find that Hekate's energy is more readily available. The Liminal Realm is the energetic world where the Under World, Middle World and Upper World meet. This is the center of Hekate's power. It can be thought of as her home. We can travel to the Liminal Realm when we want to stand fully in Her power. The initiation ritual at the end of this book will take you to this location. While traveling to this realm is a very occasional adventure, every evening we voyage to the dream world where we tap into the broader liminal realm between reality and metaphysical experience. As humans, we experience the Liminal Realm as the astral plane or the Other World. It is the domain of metaphysical experiences, including the dream world.

Exercise: Intentional Lucid Dreaming

Intentional lucid dreaming opens the portal between us and the Liminal Realm so that we can receive powerful messages from Hekate, the other deities we work with, the spirit realm, our ancestors and other metaphysical forces. Lucid dreaming refers to the broad category of dreams where we experience awareness while asleep. It's quite different from doing a metaphysical journey where we are awake but have purposefully entered an altered state of consciousness using meditative techniques. In dream work, the altered state of consciousness naturally arises because we are asleep.

Lucid Dreaming and the Energetic Realms

The Other World is the energetic realm available for humans to travel in. If you are a practitioner of Modern Hekatean Witchcraft, it is the human equivalent to the Liminal Realm where Hekate abides. Thus, the Other World is the energetic liminal space between our mundane Middle World and the energetic realms including the Liminal Realm, the Upper World and the Under World. The Middle World itself is an energetic realm, too. The energy of this realm consists of our own energy and the forces from the other realms that connect us to them. Think of the Other World as purely energetic landscape of the Middle World. Within this framework, dreaming becomes a portal to this Other World. We can time travel, journey to the energetic realms and communicate with the inhabitants of the realms.

How Intentional Lucid Dreaming Works

Lucid dreaming is a great way to gain insight into the realms, the deities, other metaphysical forces and ourselves. In intentional lucid dreaming, we use our power of the mind to chart a course through the dreamscape, so we can receive very specific messages from the realms. This can be a response to a question that you want answered. The more precise our intention, the greater the likelihood of receiving wisdom about our query. You can set the intention to receive a message from Hekate during your intentional lucid dream.

Guidelines for Intentional Lucid Dreaming

There are different ways to go about lucid dreaming. You may experience the dream soon after you retire for the night or you may wake up from the dream during your sleep. The important thing is to get into a relaxed state after you get into bed while holding your intention foremost in your mind.

Get to Know Your Dream World

Write about your dreams for at least a few weeks so you can determine the dominant themes, characters, and emotions you feel. You can make note of how chaos and control play out in your dreams.

Set Your Intention

You need to be very clear about what it is you hope to achieve. Start with your general idea and then narrow it down. Once you have your intention developed, it's helpful to write your dream intention on a piece of paper and place it under your pillow. Your intention can be to have an encounter with a deity or entity or you can seek specific guidance about one area. For example, your intention could be to have Hekate show you the way to further develop your psychic abilities. You can also ask for answers to mundane questions, such as "what do I need to do to make more money?"

Select Correspondences

Hekate's epithets, herbs, colors, crystals, symbols and other correspondences can be incorporated into your intention to enhance its power. You can use color magic by using ink in a hue that corresponds to your intention. Blue is associated with communication, so it's entirely appropriate for writing the intention. Hekate is associated with black, red and white. These are also the dominant colors of witchcraft.

Write Your Script

Expand your intention into a point-form script. Include the characters, themes, locations, your emotions, etc. You need to think about the script several times before attempting to use it for lucid dreaming. Review the script at least a couple of times during the day before your intentional lucid dreaming experience.

Using Herbs to Support Your Intentional Lucid Dreaming

Another way to boost your connection to the Other World is by placing herbs in a sachet under your pillow or close to your sleeping area. Suitable herbs for intentional lucid dreaming include a blend of lavender, mugwort and sage. Lavender will help you stay in the dream state, while mugwort will open your psychic abilities. Sage will support these other two herbs while protecting you from unwanted visitors in the Other World.

Salt placed beside the bedside or in a separate sachet under the pillow helps to ensure a beneficial lucid dream experience. In addition, you can wrap your intention around the salt, so that the salt will collect the dream for you making it easier to recall.

Scheduling Your Intentional Lucid Dream Experience

To provide the best experience, you should consider the lunar phases and astrological conditions when scheduling your dreamwork. These factors may not interfere with your experience, but you should take note of them and factor them into your planning and your processing of the dream afterwards. You should also record the day of the week because different symbolic energies are associated with each one. These symbols can show up in dreamwork.

Preparing for the Intentional Lucid Dream Experience

On the day that you plan to have your intentional lucid dream experience, you should prepare the herbs, salt and write your intention on a piece of paper. Make sure that your sleeping area is tidy. If you are planning on having an experience with a specific deity, you should have a representation of them – either an image or one of their symbols – either in or under your pillow or beside your bed. Make an offering to them at bedtime. Avoid heavy meals, caffeine and alcohol for twelve hours before your planned bedtime on the day that you'll be doing your dreamwork. Sex should be postponed, too. All these things can interfere with your natural abilities to cross into the Other World and your psychic skills at receiving messages from the energetic realms.

Relaxation techniques, such as a ritual bath or meditation is indicated to relieve stress and worries before bedtime. While intention lucid dreaming may still occur, it is less likely to be successful and you're much more likely to encounter nasty beings if you are in an agitated state. You want that calm but alert feeling you create through relaxation techniques to flow into your lucid dreaming. This will enable you to pay attention to the dream better.

Write About Your Intention Lucid Dream

As soon as possible after the dream, journal about it. Dream messages often come to us in riddles and symbols. Writing about them can help us unravel their meanings. If you are using intentional lucid dreaming for metaphysical work, avoid doing so more than once a month. This is very intense work that can take time to process.

Dream Processing

1. Record immediately upon awaking all the details of the dream that you remember. Using the voice memo function on your phone is a great tool for doing this or summarize the dream in your journal.
2. Processing the dream should occur soon after awakening, but can wait until later, especially if you made a recording.

Prompts for processing:
- What is my current emotional state? (You'll carry the dom-

inant feelings of the dream over into the waking world.)

- Who appeared in my dream?
- What were the activities that I was doing?
- What were the other characters doing?
- What did I say?
- What did the other characters say?
- What were the symbols? (This can include many things. Dreams are notoriously cryptic, look for colors, things associated with the deities you wanted to connect with, animal messengers, etc.)
- What happened? (Did you go on a journey? Sit on a throne? Fly?)
- What time period was it? (Past, present, future.)
- What do I think the dream meant?
- What am I being asked to do in waking life?

3. Interpretation: Now that you've processed the dream, you should move on to your interpretation of it. You should start with your understanding, write it down and then seek other sources, such as a standard dream interpretation guide.

4. Follow up:

- If there was something you were asked to do in the dream, make a plan and then get busy.
- Be gentle with yourself for the day after the dream experience. The emotions of the dream may carry forward into your waking life. Take time to notice these feelings and release them if they don't serve you well.
- Pay attention for symbols and other messages that reinforce your dream experience during the days afterwards.

Using the Energy of Locations
Locations have their own unique energy, whether it's a busy

city intersection or a meeting of three paths in a secluded park. When planning a rite at a crossroads, determine how the energy of a specific location will factor into what you are doing. Determine if there are natural correspondences of Hekate in the environment. For example, oak is sacred to Hekate, so finding a three-way crossroads with an oak tree nearby can be considered very special. If you are working with Hekate as Guardian, you may want to find a crossroads that reflects Under World energy. Finally, you can add lunar energy to the location by planning your ritual during a suitable part of the moon phase. You can bring items to the crossroads to heighten the energy by selecting from the correspondences discussed earlier. I generally do my workings at the crossroads of land, sea and sky because I live right on the coast and have access to remote places free from the built environment.

If you can't easily get to such a place, you can use the end of your driveway as a three-way crossroads and do your workings there. If this isn't available for you, then create your own indoor three-way crossroads using dirt from such a location. This can be done either as part of your altar, or you can create a temporary one. To do the latter, lay a black cloth on the floor and then arrange your crossroads. When you are finished with your working, you can bundle it up and store the portable crossroads until you need it again. You know by now that the cloth and dirt should be magically prepared before use. Store the dirt in a clean container that you leave outside or near a windowsill if it has come from a high-traffic area. If you appropriated the dirt from a secluded crossroads, then it is most likely fine to use right away. You'll be able to tell if the dirt is ready for magic or placing on your altar.

Practice: Deipnon Crossroads Offering
I don't think you've truly experienced the Deipnon until you've placed your offerings at a three-way crossroads. Choose your

place wisely, you don't want to cause an uproar or threaten local wildlife. Record the location and other details in your Book of Shadows. Perhaps you found an appropriate place on your Correspondence Quest. I know that this exercise can be intimidating, so determine your comfort level and act accordingly. You can perform the ritual in your home at your altar with the offerings on it and then leave them at the crossroads. Or you can do the entire working at your crossroads. Sundown is the most appropriate time to leave your offering, but don't put yourself at risk. After you finish the ritual, record your experiences in your journal and update the entry in your Book of Shadows.

Creating Sacred Space

Sacred space is created using objects and tools and by harnessing energy. There are two ways we create sacred space. The first is by creating a special location featuring objects representative of Hekate. We make an altar as a way of expressing our devotion to Hekate and as a focal point for our magical activities. The second way we create sacred space is when we contain the natural energies into a magical circle. This circle is often created with our altar. You've had the experiences of creating an altar and casting the circle so far in this course. Now, with all that you've learned since then, it's time to complete your altar and cast a powerful energetic space.

Exercise: Completing Your Altar

It takes some time to prepare all the items for the altar, especially if you need to buy or make items. I suggest that you read the next section and then make a plan. You should complete your altar on the Full Moon. You've been creating your altar throughout this book with the exercises that you've completed. By now, you have the basic altar including the Salt Strophalos and an image of Hekate. Each of these things represent one of the four core components of an altar:

- Representations of Hekate
- Hekate's Symbols
- Correspondences
- Tools
- Personal items

Representations of Hekate

The heart of your altar is the representation of Hekate that you have chosen. You may already own a statue of Our Lady or you may have been using a favorite image as part of your workings so far in this book. While there are many beautiful statues available, having one is not necessary. You can continue to use the image that you've been working with or use another one. Many devotees make their own statues and images. I think the things we make are especially favored by Hekate. There are so many ways to make your own image. If you are artistic you can paint or sculpt your own. You can use a photo editor to customize an existing image. Be creative.

Your altar should have one main representation of Hekate on it, placed at the back in the middle. There should be space enough around it to place your offerings. The image you'll be featuring on your altar should be prepared for use by anointing it and offering it to Hekate. In some traditions, these images are ensouled with the energies of the deity being worked with. I don't believe that we can forcibly make Hekate contain even a tiny bit of her energy into anything. However, we can anoint the image of Her that we choose for our altar and see Her blessing upon it.

Preparing a Sacred Image for Use on the Altar

The image should be cleansed of any nonessential energy in the same way that you've prepared other things for workings – place it on the Salt Strophalos. The salt will capture all the energy that is on the image. After the image is cleansed, pass it through the smoke of the Three Keys incense if you are able. If not, anointing the statue with magical water made from the incense will be sufficient. To anoint the image, either after purifying with smoke or without, cleanse yourself first, then place three drops of the water at the top of the image. Slowly rub the water all over the image, adding more as you go. If you are using a paper image, you can use the incense in the dry form. As you are anointing the image, say:

> Hail Hekate, I anoint this image in your honor.
> This is an expression of my devotion.
> Hail Hekate, I anoint this image in your honor.
> May it be a portal to Your mysteries,
> Hail Hekate, I anoint this image in your honor.
> My intentions are true and my will is strong.

After you've finished anointing the image, kiss it and give it your own personal blessing. Now sit it on the place where it will stay. If you work with other deities, it's probably best to keep them out of your Hekatean altar until after you have completed your Initiation at the end of this book.

Symbols

You already have the Salt Strophalos as a symbol of Hekate. This should be kept to the left of your image. On the right you'll place your Key of Initiation after you complete this course. In front of Hekate place three candles representing Her fires. The strophalos represents Hekate as Guide, the candles are symbolic of Hekate as Guardian and the Key of Initiation will complete the triad as a reflection of Hekate as Gatekeeper. Dress the candles using the techniques outlined in the incense making exercise. Also use the steps from that exercise to prepare the candles if you don't have black, red and white ones.

Correspondences

The candles already represent the color correspondences. You can add pieces of quartz, obsidian and jasper, too. I have small bowls of incense on my altar. Incense should be kept on the opposite side of the salt. You can have a representation of each of the Three Realms. This would include something dead (bones), something stagnant (water or wine) and something growing (a small plant or clippings, even a bulb of garlic). The dead object represents Hekate as Guardian and Under World energy. The stagnant, or balanced, object is for Hekate as the Way and Middle World energy. The "fresh" object is for Hekate of the Upper World and Gatekeeper. These objects should be arranged in correspondence with the appropriate candle. If you are using crossroads dirt, you can put a bit of that in for the Middle World. Hekate as Queen of Land, Sea and Sky is represented using a bit of dirt, purified water (salt water is best) and a feather. Again, arrange these objects in correspondence with the others on your altar. Place your Tarot deck on the same side as the incense. Add whatever additional correspondences that you feel led to, but just make sure that they are prepared in your Salt Strophalos or purified by the moon.

Tools

Placing tools on your altar is done because the altar is imbued with sacred energy, so it keeps them ready for use without you having to prepare them before each working. The three tools are the feather, the sword and the wand. The feather (as previously mentioned) represents Hekate of the Upper World. The sword is Hekate's weapon alongside Guide that She shares with us for use in our magic. The wand represents Her fires and the Under World. The feather is used in creating magical space and for fanning our sacred smoke over ourselves, our space and the objects we used. The end of the feather should be wrapped to make it easy to hold on to, preferably using black, red and white ribbon or leather strips. The same should be done for your blade. The wand can be any stick of your liking or a purchased one. The wood should be of a tree sacred to Hekate, such as almond, oak, bay laurel, or yew.

In addition to these tools, you should have a special bowl and chalice for offerings in front of Hekate's image. Prepare your tools and the bowl in the same manner as everything else.

Personal items

The last things to go on the altar are representative of who you are. It can be a picture, a lock of your hair or a piece of jewelry; it doesn't matter if it is something that is highly connected to you energetically. Put this item directly in front of Hekate's image as a symbol of your devotion.

Practice: Cleansing the Salt Strophalos

Before doing any workings at your altar, now is the time to cleanse and recharge the salt in the strophalos. Remove the salt from its tray by pouring it into a clean container. Return the tray to the altar. You can have a second batch of salt ready to replace or wait for that salt to be cleansed and recharged. The "used" salt should be placed outside if possible or near a window for three nights under the waxing moon. Then the salt can be returned to the tray. Now that your tools are ready, you can use them to create the Hekate's Wheel in the salt. This is the last stage in preparing your altar. It's ready to use.

Creating Energetic Sacred Space

The first use of your altar will be as your starting point for an energetic sacred space. While the altar is an energetic space, it is limited in size. You can't crawl onto your altar to do a working. When doing your daily working (like prayers and chanting), the energy being emitted from the altar is sufficient. However, when you are doing a full working, you need to create a space large enough to completely encircle you. The purposes of this energetic circle are to:

- Increase your focus and power
- Create a portal for evoking Hekate
- Summon the energy of the correspondences and items used in a working
- Contain and blend these energies in one space
- Protect you from outside energies

There are many ways to create this space. You may already be familiar with casting a magical circle. In Modern Hekatean Witchcraft, the power of this circle is enhanced through the technique of Casting Hekate's Wheel.

Exercise: Casting Hekate's Wheel

The strophalos, or Hekate's Wheel, is a fantastic symbol to use for creating a sacred circle. You're already familiar with how powerful it is for purifying objects. Now you'll experience this power as you create a sacred circle using it. I recommend studying your Salt Strophalos while you create the circle for the first few times. It may take a while to get the technique down pat.

Preparations

Prepare yourself by cleansing and dress in clean, comfortable clothing (preferably all black or sky clad, so your clothing won't interfere in the casting). Sweep or vacuum the area around your altar. Your altar is already prepared.

Casting Hekate's Wheel

Once you are ready, standing before your altar, do the Three Keys Chant until you feel relaxed and ready. Then, take up the feather, blade and wand. Take three big steps back from your altar but remain facing it.

Summoning and Exaltation:

> Hail Hekate,
> I call upon the energy of your great wheel
> To sanctify this space.
> Hekate World Soul,
> Hail Hekate, Guardian,
> Hail Hekate, Guide,
> Hail Hekate, Gatekeeper.
> Bless this sacred space
> With your mighty presence.
> Make available to me
> Your energy for this sacred circle.

Envision the energy pouring out of your image of Hekate and the correspondences. See these energies as black, red and white. Take some time here to really envision these three distinct but connected energy streams.

Casting the Inner Circle

Once you are firmly connected to the streams, begin to cast the strophalos. Visualize yourself standing on the six-rayed figure in the middle of the strophalos. You become this figure. Each ray represents part of you: your head, your arms, your torso and your legs. At the heart of the figure (which is you) is your soul-spark. This is your higher self and the first circle of Hekate's Circle. Within this lies the energy of Hekate as the World Soul, where the three streams of energy combine. Envision the energy streams flowing in and out of this core.

Holding the three objects in your left hand, extend your right arm out. Make a complete circle around yourself while saying, "I am sovereign, safe and secure within this circle." This circle contains your energy, but it acts like a permeable membrane through which you can easily draw upon energies outside of your circle. Remember that you can retreat into this space if you feel overwhelmed by the energies in the outer circles. This is your space, the second circle of Hekate's Wheel. Say:

Hail Hekate,
I am your sovereign child,
Free to do as I will,
But seeking your presence
And guidance.

Creating the Serpent

Next, it's time to create the serpent. This serpent is the symbol of all life. It is a representation of Hekate as the World Soul with Her aspects as Guardian, Guide and Gatekeeper all represented. As such, you are going to call upon each of Her major energy currents – Under World, Upper World, and Middle World. You can also think of these currents as sea (black), sky (white), and land (red).

Each coil is going to represent one of these realms. When unified, the snake will hold energy of all things. The black coil is for the underworld, land of emotions. The white coil is for the upper world, realm of the intellect. The red coil unites them both in the middle world, the land of actions. You will remain sovereign because of the circle around you.

You're going to make each of the three coils just outside of your sovereign circle. The "tops" of each segment of the coils will remain open until you close them. We'll get to that part. First, let's go over creating each coil.

Casting the Black Coil

When you are ready, begin to expand the black, red and white energy streams that flow through you; let them envelope you and reach out beyond your individual circle. Feel the circle expand so that you are surrounded with these energies. Now let them pierce your circle; they reach out beyond you now. Through your feet, pull up the energy of the Under World to cast the black coil of the serpent. Say:

I call Hekate as Guardian,
And upon the energy of the Under World,
The depths of the seas,
The world of emotion,
May mine be true,
And this space sacred.

Place the wand in your left hand. The wand connects to this energy stream. Draw the first coil of the serpent in the middle circle of Hekate's Wheel. You are connected to this stream now. Place the wand beside your left foot.

Casting the White Coil

Next, take the feather in your right hand, putting the blade in your left. Envision the energy of the Upper World emanating from your soul, reaching out to the realm of intellect. Say:

I call upon Hekate as Gatekeeper,
And the energy of the Upper World,
The skies above,
The world of will,
May mine be strong.
And this space sacred.

Draw the Upper World coil of the serpent on your right side using the feather. You are now connected to this energy stream. Place the feather beside your right foot.

Casting the Red Coil

Next, hold the blade with both hands at your heart center. Feel the life force, the red of the Middle World reach out through you into the blade as it absorbs the energy of the world of action all around you. Say:

I call upon Hekate as Guide
And the energy of the Middle World,
And the land of everyday existence,
The world of actions,
May mine be wise
And this space sacred.

Draw the third coil of the serpent, that of the Middle World, in front of you with both hands on the blade.

Unifying the Serpent

Hold your hands high and close the tops of the coils together with your blade, so that the energy from each coil merges into the other two. Spin as you do this, creating an active energy force. Feel the energy of the snake going through you, connecting you to Hekate:

Hail Hekate,
The Great Serpent that is all of life,
Welcome to this sacred space.

Casting the Outer Circle

Now that the serpent is complete, feel the three energy streams around you. Separate, but connected into the serpent of creation. The black and white energies come together with the red in your blade. Hold the blade up with both hands, then down with both hands and return to your heart center. Say:

Blessed Hekate, She Above All,
Close Your sacred Wheel,
Be here with me.
Hear my words.

You are now fully contained within the third circle of Hekate's Wheel.

Hekate's Wheel is Cast
Now, the strophalos is fully cast. Envision it spinning if it doesn't make you dizzy! Take some time to acknowledge Hekate:

Hail Hekate,
Accept my gratitude
For Your presence.

In the future, this is where you'll move into your ritual. For now, the casting is complete.

Opening Hekate's Wheel
When you finish with the ritual, open your space.

Opening the Outer Circle
Start by asking Hekate to open the outer circle: Blessed Hekate, thank you for your presence, open this circle.

Opening the Serpent
Next release each of the coils of the serpent, starting with the Upper World: Blessed Hekate, thank You for Your presence, I release the white coil of the Upper World. Take the feather in your right hand and sweep the coil away. Take the wand in your left hand: *Blessed Hekate, thank You for Your presence, I release the black coil of the Under World.* Sweep away the black coil with the wand. Put down the wand and the feather. Finally, hold the

blade with both hands at your heart center: *Blessed Hekate, thank You for Your presence, I release the red coil of the Middle World.*

Releasing Yourself

Keeping the blade at your heart center, envision the circle around you being absorbed back into your body: *I release myself from this sacred space, my intention is pure, my actions are true and my will is strong.* Envision your bodily energy that you connected to each ray of the central figure returning into you. The strophalos is open. You can finish up by saying whatever you feel led to.

Other Ways to Create Energetic Sacred Space

Casting Hekate's Wheel is a powerful tool for focusing our attention, harnessing natural energies and getting Hekate's attention, but you may not always have the time or need to use it. There are many other ways to cast the circle.

Ritual Sweeping

One technique that is quite easy and that I often use is ritual sweeping. The broom, as you know, is one of the most potent symbols of the witch. Many of us have special ones – called besoms – that are used solely for magical purposes, such as ritual sweeping. Personally, I find this sweeping technique is appropriate for doing workings that require more than my daily devotional work, but less than a full-blown ritual or spell. Begin the usual way, by preparing the broom, yourself and the space. You can dress the broom the same way you do candles – with salt, magical water or oils. In addition, you can purchase a besom, make your own, or use a regular (but new) inexpensive broom. It's very much the intention that counts in all of witchcraft, and ritual sweeping is no different. Decorating your besom with correspondences will make it even more powerful. The sweeping technique is simple: starting at your altar, sweep a clockwise circle three times while chanting our daily mantra (Welcome … Hekate, Guardian, Hekate, Guide, Hekate Gatekeeper … Welcome … Hekate, Guardian … and so on). Envision that the energetic "dust" stirred up by the besom creates a cone of power, encompassing you and your altar. When you are finished with your working, open the circle with three rotations counter clockwise, chanting again but saying "farewell" instead of "welcome."

It is a good idea to practice these techniques for a few weeks until you get comfortable with them because casting a circle – whether it's Hekate's Wheel or through ritual sweeping – is an integral part of all workings. It's best to match the type of circle you'll cast to the nature of your working. For daily prayers and meditations, lighting candles on your altar are sufficient. For workings like intentional prayers, you want to ensure that you center and ground yourself prior to the working and connect to your altar through candle or incense lighting. When it comes to formal rituals, such as highly structured spells or honorific rituals, you should take the time to cast the strophalos, especially if you'll be evoking Hekate. Follow your intuition and these guidelines when you are deciding what level of sacred space is necessary for any working.

Summary

There are many different types of sacred space associated with Hekate. Naturally sacred locations are liminal zones, particularly the three-way crossroads. Liminal times of day such as dawn and twilight are especially powerful for connecting to Hekate. In addition to liminal spaces and times, Hekate holds dominion over land, sea and sky. From this perspective, the entire earth is Her sacred realm. Her reign extends over the three energetic realms of the Under World, the Middle World and the Upper World. The inner sanctum of Hekate lies in the Liminal Realm where these three realms meet. The Liminal Realm is the mystical world that is mostly out of reach to us, except through spiritual work. We can travel to this Realm using various techniques, such as intentional lucid dreaming. Created sacred space includes altars and energetic circles. The major parts of the altar include an image of Hekate, Her symbols, correspondences, tools and a personal item representing our position in the center of our practice. Energetic sacred space is created by casting a circle using Hekate's Wheel.

Lesson 13: Spell Crafting

Recite what you wish, and it will happen ...
(*PGM,* Spell to the Waning Moon, pp. 633–731)

If only spell casting was that simple! If you've read *The Greek Magical Papyri,* you know that the little snippet above doesn't reflect the complex ingredients and detailed recitations featured in the spells in this ancient collection of magical workings. In this lesson, we explore the art and science of spell crafting.

Practice: Deipnon and Noumenia Work

Are you keeping up with the monthly honoring of Hekate on the Dark Moon? How's it going? What about Noumenia? Ideally, you should be starting this lesson around the same time as these two events. Don't forget to record these rituals in your Book of Shadows. By now, your Witch's Hour of Power should be an established part of your daily routine.

It's about Power: The Point of Witchcraft

Like the line from that ancient spell, the point of witchcraft can be simplified into a few words, but the meaning of them is as intricate as a spider's web. The point of witchcraft: to control outcomes. All of witchcraft is about manipulating energies to influence an outcome in favor of what we desire. Control requires power. All of witchcraft is about power. We seek power using correspondences and petitioning Hekate to intervene. However, these are external power sources. The greatest energy available to use comes from our internal power plant.

Therefore, this course started with lots of information and exercises about personal development and why we do the practices that make up our Witch's Hour of Power. Because there is no separation between our witchery and who we are. If our lives are a mess, so are our spells. If we have no personal power – known as agency – then we can't expect to exert control in workings. Living a magical life helps us to function in our own best interests, to stand in our personal power and to be a guide for others. Exercises that develop our mindfulness skills through meditation, balancing, grounding and centering, reinforce this force by helping us retain our sovereign power. Then we worked on our relationship with Hekate, both in terms of our personal understanding and through the literature extant. Through devotional acts we acknowledge both Her power and our own. Because we recognize that even the most powerful witch can use a little help, we've studied the power of the correspondences. Plus, we don't want to ask for more of Hekate than what we can accomplish ourselves through other means. Part of this means learning to utilize Her energy through our daily Tarot practice, serving to further strengthen our connection with Her and our own magical abilities. Then we moved onto discussing the types and importance of those very powerful sacred spaces, and how to create an energetic one. Everything in this course has been a lesson in power, specifically the application of our energies, Hekate's and correspondences for our own purposes. That's witchcraft. Now, it's time to turn our attention to the art and science of writing your own spells.

Before moving on to the discussion about types of witchcraft, I want to add a bit more about power. Part of standing in our own power is knowing that there are times when we must surrender it. Wisdom is knowing when to do this. We can surrender a problem to Hekate when we have exhausted all our own methods. Placing it in Her capable hands, we can trust that the outcome will be for our highest good. At the personal level, we can learn to accept things as is. Acceptance is one of the most powerful tools available to us. We waste a lot of time and energy trying to change things that even the very mighty witches, that we are, can't change; or can't invest the amount of energy necessary to make it happen. It takes wisdom to discern when a situation requires acceptance or resistance. When faced with a problem, we need to explore these concepts before settling down to spell crafting.

Understanding: Exploring Acceptance and Resistance

We demonstrate personal power when we choose to accept or resist any problem that we are facing. One thing that's a complete waste of time to resist is the past. It's already happened. You can't change it. When we are still controlled by traumatic experiences we are not truly standing in our power. When we cling to the idea – resist the truth – that things could have been different, we're stuck. Not only does this interfere with acting in our own best interests, it greatly diminishes our witch-power. Before you begin your work as a highly-skilled spell crafter, you should reflect upon things in your life that you may be resisting, especially painful experiences. Accepting that these things happened will remove them as barriers between living your truth and becoming a fantastic witch.

Even if you are highly gifted at witchery naturally, resistance to that which we cannot change will prevent you from developing your skills to their full potential. I've heard so many stories, including my own, of spells that manifested exactly what the practitioner hoped, only to find that it just led to more hurt. What is it you need to let go of? One way to sort this out – if you don't already know – is by observing how you allocate the time given to various people. Do you think about your ex all the time? What could you be thinking about instead? Concentrate on replacing feelings of hurt with positive ones. Take at least a couple of days to contemplate and write about things that you need to let go of. Make a list. Then burn it. You just wrote and completed a potent spell.

Ancient Hekatean Witchcraft

The exercise on acceptance is an example of how different our contemporary perspective on witchcraft (and Hekate) is in comparison with the ancients. However, there is a lot of information to be gained through studying the historical texts. One thing that emerges is that much of spell crafting was about cursing. Not all ancient Hekatean witchcraft was malevolent in nature, though. In the famous tales about Jason and the Argonauts, Medea was initially seen as helpful:

> There is a maiden, nurtured in the halls of Aeetes, whom the goddess Hecate taught to handle magic herbs with exceeding skill all that the land and flowing waters produce. With them is quenched the blast of unwearied flame, and at once she stays the course of rivers as they rush roaring on and checks the stars and the paths of the sacred moon.[46]

However, Medea turned out to be the opposite of an innocent maiden, and later used her Hekatean witchcraft to cause all sorts of damage. Another witch that involved Hekate in magical destruction was Simaetha. In Theocritus' second Idyll, she uses bay leaves in a potent love spell (of sorts, it's complicated) evoking Hekate: "Delphis has brought me pain, and I burn this bay leaf against Delphis. As it crackles in the flames with a sharp noise and flares leaving no trace of ash, so may Delphis' body melt in the flame."[47]

Goals of Witchcraft

Now as then, Hekate will support our witchcraft, whether it's for nefarious purposes or for the highest good. While we are probably not going to be focused on making people suffer to the same extent as the ancient witches, we approach witchcraft in basically the same way: using our power to control outcomes through Hekate's help and the use of correspondences. Even the subjects of our spells haven't changed much since the days of Medea and Simaetha – we want to attract good things, protect ourselves from the bad and heal others. The basic tools of witchcraft haven't changed all that much, either. Nor have the correspondences that we use. However, our understanding of healing and evil spirits can be quite different from theirs. We often seek emotional healing for ourselves. And the evil spirits we face are typically of the human kind. Nevertheless, the goals of witchcraft are very similar – we seek to bring about a desired outcome and we ask Hekate for our help. That last point is an important one in Modern Hekatean Witchcraft. In other approaches, it is believed that the practitioner can manipulate the deity they involve in a working. In Modern Hekatean Witchcraft, just like we are sovereign beings, so is Hekate. We can petition for Her favor, but there's no way to control a goddess as powerful as She is.

Spell Categories

Up until this point in the course, we've been exploring energy work that petitions Hekate without doing an actual spell. The difference is that a spell consists of a multi-pronged all-out approach. We use words, correspondences, movements (e.g., hand signals) and petition Hekate.

Attraction and Removal

In all spells, we are trying to bring something towards us or push it away. Even though our spells often involve trying to attract our desired outcome, just as common are the spells we do to push things away from us. The main goal of witchcraft is thus divided into these two broad categories of attraction and repulsion. Our spells use one or both goals. We can further divide the two categories into the types of spells that we do. General attraction workings can benefit from the use of clover and tourmaline. Work with Hekate's Upper World energy as

201

Gatekeeper or World Soul. Under World Hekate, Guardian and Dark Mother are currents appropriate for all types of removal magick. Yarrow and garnet are great correspondences with this type of working. Attraction magick is best done under the waxing moon, while removal spells are suited to the waning.

Abundance

Attraction spells often focus on creating an abundance of the spell object (i.e., prosperity), but not always. For example, if I am hoping to attract a romantic partner, I probably don't want an abundance of them! Abundance is a bountiful state where there is more than enough of the object to meet your needs. It's best represented by the Ace of Cups, where literally the cup is overflowing. Seek Hekate as *Ergatis* (Energizer) to strengthen your abundance workings which can be further enhanced with pine and malachite.

Banishing

There are times when we need to completely remove something from our lives, whether it's a bad habit or a toxic person. Banishing spells use correspondences that remove our connection to the problem and then send it away, using two types of repulsion magic. Cord cutting magic is often a highly effective technique for banishing. Use correspondences appropriate for your specific situation. Using the poisons, like aconite and belladonna, are recommended for banishing, but only if you are confident in handling them. Let's be clear that you're using the energy of these plants to "kill" your relationship with the focus, not actually poisoning them. There are several ways to work with poisons, from burning them as incense to crushing their seeds. A general banishing technique is to take an image of the person or problem, rip it up and grind in one of the recommended poisons in a mortar and pestle reserved for toxic workings. Put the toxic mixture into a black bag while wearing gloves. Cover your altar with a disposable black cloth, such as a scrap of material. Light a black candle and burn the Three Keys incense. Write a script specific for your banishment, perhaps petitioning Hekate as Guardian to burn their connection to you. Banishing is Under World work. Make sure to include a section on cutting all cords with the person. Using a real piece of cord, preferably black, tie one end to the toxic bag and hold the other one. While saying your script, cut this cord with scissors. When you're finished, wrap up the bag and the string in the piece of fabric. You should dispose of the bag as far away from your property as possible. That's just one example of a banishing spell template. Make a black salt from ashes, charcoal and sea salt. Cast your enemies off by throwing it to the wind while reciting their names. Summon the energy of Hekate the Fearful (*Phoberos*) to help banish the unwanted.

Binding

Binding can refer to containing energy within an object or a person, or to creating an energetic cord between us and something else. Binding needs to be carefully considered. When properly done, binding is very challenging to undo. Bay laurel is a powerful herb of attraction, and Hekate as Guide is often suitable for spells where we want to bind someone to us. Roses are another great ingredient for a binding spell. Take the three colors of Hekate and one for you and one for the person or object to which you wish to be bound. Soak the ribbons or strings in the mixture of bay laurel and rose water until you are ready to do the spell. Wrap them in parchment paper and wring them out, reserving the water and keeping the paper. Once the ribbons and paper are dried, write the script of your spell on the paper and braid the ribbon while reciting it. Then roll up the paper and wrap the braid around it. Birch and onyx are powerful aids for binding.

Growth

A growth spells focuses on planting the seeds of a project to manifest it successfully. Growth spells are usually done at the beginning of a project and include elements specific to that project so that we attract all that we need to be successful. Doing a growth spell for a new business is an example. Mighty Hekate (*Kyria*) can be petitioned for growth and other kinds of attraction magick. Olive oil is a great base for a growth potion. Combine with herbs suited for what you are manifesting. Let rest for one moon cycle then anoint an image of what you are growing under the full moon. Add a piece of turquoise to further strengthen the potion.

Healing

The things we seek Hekate's problem solving assistance for often concern physical and emotional healing. Healing is one of the core activities of the witch. A lot of our efforts concern healing ourselves, but we are also called to support others in their recovery attempts. We can use intentional prayer wherein we petition Hekate to bring about healing, we can create a healing altar and include names, we can send distance healing, or we can engage in hands-on energetic techniques. Regardless of which approach you use, I recommend always having the consent of the individual that you are interceding for except when praying for their general good health and fortune. For hands-on healing, I recommend training in an energetic technique such as Reiki or Quantum Touch prior to getting into this business. If you are responding to a distance healing request, you can write the person's name on a piece of paper and place it on your altar. There's so much power in a name and the written word. Hekate as Healer (*Paionios*) can be called upon to guide and support your healing workings. Juniper and agate are excellent correspondences.

Manifestation

Most of our magic is about manifesting something – whether it's to manifest a close relationship through binding or for curing someone. Manifestation has come to be seen as specific to making material objects appear in recent times – money, jobs, houses, etc. A manifesting potion can be made using the Three Keys Magical Water as a base then oak (bark, essence, leaves, oil) and a piece of amethyst. Finally, include your own hair to keep the energy personal. To use this potion in a simple spell, make a detailed list about what you want (be sure to copy it in your Book of Shadows first) and then put it in the potion. Mix in a symbol of what it is you want. Often, we can use a key for this. Seal the jar until you ready to manifest what you are after. Open it and place it by the window or outside after opening.

Mediumship

If you are interested in communicating with a departed loved one, you can petition Hekate as Guardian to bring the person forward to you. Add to this petition an incense of Under World herbs (such as yarrow) that include those connected to the dead and for protection. You can unintentionally attract unwanted visitors from the other side when you are working with the other side, so protection is a must (black salt; sage). If you're new to mediumship work, I recommend using the Tarot as the medium through which the messages are delivered. Call upon Hekate as Guardian, Guide and Gatekeeper for mediumship work.

Protection

I mentioned protection in the last paragraph on mediumship workings, but there are many other circumstances requiring this sort of spell work. Examples include safeguarding yourself and others from harm and protecting your belongings. A simple spell consists of writing a script and then envisioning a protective shield around whatever it is you need to safeguard. Sage is an excellent herb of protection. Ash, poplar and rowan (all basically the same energy) can be used to draw a protective circle. Make a charm from a key and a chunk of fluorite to carry with you for protection from everyday hassles and harms. Usually a protection working is added to any banishment spell because you can't be too careful. Hekate as Guardian can be counted on for protection, so include this role in any working of this type.

Psychic Development

Psychic development refers more to abilities than a specific type of working. However, we can cast spells that will help enhance our psychic skills, including opening our third eye, astral travel and divination. Psychic development spells are classified as attraction magic and Upper World energy. Turn to the Keeper of the Keys to reveal the mysteries. Adding elm and sodalite will increase psychic abilities.

Reversal

Sometimes we need more than protection from a toxic person; we need to reverse their energy that they are directing towards us (or another) back at them. This is the purest form of reversal magic, and usually accompanies a protection spell and banishment. However, there are times when we cannot banish a person from our lives, but we can reverse their harmful energies back at them. While this technique is highly practical in our everyday lives, it's also well-applied to when we feel that we are under psychic attack from another person or even a malicious entity. Betony, Datura and Devil's Trumpet are all excellent for reversal magic. If you aren't banishing the person or object, you can still do the cord cutting part of the spell discussed earlier. In your script, make it clear that you are petitioning Hekate (in an Under World capacity) to not only remove them from your life but for their harmful deeds to reflect upon them. This type of spell is a last resort, after your problem-solving skills, protection spells and everything else fails. There are many types of reversal magic beyond this one example. A selenite wand can be used to reverse energy. Hemlock can accomplish the same task.

Transmutation

Unlike reversal magic where the point is to send energy back at something, when we do a transmutation spell we are changing the energy within a person or an object. I had this student once who used to do a transmutation spell over her very grumpy husband every night while he slept. While I can't endorse doing magic on the unwitting, her goal was to make her own life bearable since she didn't believe that she should divorce him. Sure enough, his personality became much more positive after a month or so. Her wording was carefully chosen. Her script included turning all his cranky thoughts to happy ones. That is exactly what transmutation does. Dandelion is an excellent correspondence for transmutation workings. Opal is a suitable stone.

Those are some of the major types of spellwork. There are loads more that I haven't covered. The key thing in any spell is that you start with a very well-thought out intention. Botanicals can be used in their natural form (i.e., flower, leaf, branch, bark) or as distilled essences or essential oils. The essences, such as the Bach's flower remedies are very useful in a wide variety of workings. In addition, many are safe for internal consumption. Hemlock should never be consumed. When working with the essences, you can add almond or olive oil to make your own oil. Be mindful that some of the essences contain alcohol.

Parts of a Spell

A spell begins and ends with words. There are a few times in magic when words aren't the major focus or at least one of the main ingredients. Maybe in meditation when we are trying to calm our thoughts, but then again, trying to stop the words is all about the words. When our mundane efforts are getting us nowhere and Hekate seems disinterested in our polite petitions, it may be time for an all-out spell. Or perhaps your focus requires so much energy or is so important that you want to do a spell to ensure that you get what you're after. We've talked about the wisdom in accepting what you can't change. Given that this isn't such a situation, then let's get down to the business of constructing a spell.

Intention is Everything

I've given you some examples of different categories of spells. In each one of those when you write your own based on my recommendations, your research and intuition, you are going to start with the intention. A properly constructed intention is the most powerful part of a spell, after belief. You must be confident in your abilities to create the outcome you desire and have faith in Hekate and trust in your correspondences. Even the most carefully worded intention will fail without confidence, belief and trust. With the right wording from the outset, you can choose what "side" of Hekate that you'll be evoking, what correspondences will add to the goal and what other components are necessary. Way back near the beginning of this course, you used a word web to construct an intention. I recommend using this technique when developing any intention. I've learned that I may think I have it right, but through processing it I realize that I've forgotten something. Remember the fireplace story?

Writing the Incantation

The intention is the heart of the spell, while the incantation is the body of it. I usually record my finished intention on a new page in my Book of Shadows with the date noting the commencement of spell development. Starting with your intention in the center, construct a new word web that includes the things you need to accomplish to manifest your intention. Ask yourself what you are going to do and how you need help to achieve your goals. I use my journal to write the incantation until it is polished and then write in the Book of Shadows. When you record it in here, you can select inks that correspond to your spell. This is one flourish that I always do when recording an incantation. A great added boost comes from adding a bit of magical water to your inks.

You can write a script that includes the various things you'll be doing during the spell and other directions beside your incantation. I usually have the incantation and then the instructions underneath of it. For an incantation to be effective, you must include your own plans for manifestation. Be specific in what you're going to do. Don't ask Hekate to do something that you could possibly do yourself. It's great to ask for Her help and guidance with the activities you'll be undertaking. The incantation is spoken after sacred space is created and Hekate is evoked.

Tips for writing an incantation:

- Connect the words with correspondences.
- Use active language.
- Choose words that directly relate to the type of spell.
- Be consistent in the energy of the words.
- The structure of the incantation contains energy, too. Using rhyming techniques will enhance the energy of the spell.
- You can build an acronym reflecting your intention into the incantation to make it even more potent.

Including Hekate in the Incantation

My experience is that the more specific I am with what I'm doing the better. If you're not yet comfortable with writing your own evocation, then you have the one from earlier to use or you can adapt the other prayers and hymns used so far. Working with Hekate as Guardian, Guide and Gatekeeper is a great approach for any spell. The part of the spell script where we petition certain epithets is called the exaltation. You can use "Hail" to tug upon the cord between you and Hekate or you can use "Io" (sounds like E-o or I-o whichever is more comfortable for your tongue) which is a more traditional exaltation or begin with "Blessed." All these will get Our Lady's intention. Then commence the exaltations of the epithets. I usually start with a series of epithets connected to the spell, then add "Mistress, Attend Your Epithets!" right after, and then clearly state what I want from Her, like this:

> Hail Hekate, Guide! Hail Hekate, Gatekeeper! Hail Hekate, Energizer!
> I welcome You as Hegemonen, Propylaia and Ergatis!
> Mistress, Attend Your Epithets!
> I seek prosperity,
> Guide me towards abundance,
> Clear the way towards it,
> And lend your energy to my spell.
> My intention is true,
> My actions are wise,
> And my will is strong.

Then I would move into the incantation. I usually light a special candle to represent Hekate while summoning Her that is never connected to the spell in any other way. Black is a good color for this candle, and you can use it repeatedly in this manner.

Voces Magicae

We've talked about intention and incorporating specific aspects of Hekate into your script, but there are many other ways to incorporate words of power into a spell. Traditionally, the Voces

Magicae was a series of sounds, such as the Eleusinian Letters, that were said at the beginning of a spell. The Eleusinian Letters consist of askion, kataskion, lix, tetrax, damnameneus and aision (or aisia). They were often used in spells evoking Hekate in *The Greek Magical Papyri*. The meaning of them is unknown. There are other sounds in the *PGM* including clusters of vowels and consonants with no known meaning except as voces magicae, such as "EO IAO O KA." You can use these examples at the very beginning of your spell to focus your attention and notify your correspondences that the working is about to begin. They are typically written into the incantation. Feel free to make up your own sounds.

Other ways we can use words in spells include writing out parts of the intention, incantation, epithets and correspondences that we combine in various ways. We can also use anagrams and make sigils as stand-alone objects or as part of talismans. I have a set of tiles I made from black board that spell Hekate's name in Greek that I use for various magical things. For sigils, there are many excellent books available on making them. The basic technique is to take that one word that sums up your intention and then break it down into its lines and curves and then reconstruct them into a symbol. You can put this symbol on a magic jar or attach it to a talisman, or even just carry the sigil with you.

Correspondences

We use correspondences in spells to add energetic power. Throughout this course, you've learned about various correspondences that are strongly associated with Hekate. When we choose these items, we are both increasing the strength of the connection of the spell to Her and activating the properties of the correspondences. It's a double-whammy of spell power. However, the most important thing is to choose the correspondences that make the most sense to you. If you're not comfortable with the colors, plants and other objects that are involved in a spell, then you're likely to run into problems. I think it's vital that you craft your own spells instead of using pre-existing ones without altering them to your own style. It's always best to write the correspondences into the script to further enhance their power, such as:

Mugwort, My Lady's sacred plant,
I summon you,
This spell you now enchant.

In addition to writing the correspondences into a spell, we also activate their energetic properties during a working. There are lots of ways to do this. You can apply the technique of making magical water to your specialized blend for a spell. You can construct an incense using the selected herbs or make a sachet of them to carry with you as the spell comes to fruition. The same can be done with stones used in a spell. Stones become even more powerful if you write Voces Magicae, a symbol of Hekate or a sigil on them.

Activities

Preparing to do a spell requires quite a bit of work, but there are things to be done while you are casting the spell, too. Of course, you start with purification, creating of sacred space and evoking Hekate. But, there are parts of the incantation that often include you to do things. For example, when you come to the part of the incantation that refers to a specific correspondence, it's typical to do something with it – hold it, burn it, toss it around, etc. The way that objects are handled during a spell is another consideration. If you are doing a spell of attraction, you'll want to work with all correspondences in a clock-wise manner; the opposite is required for workings of repulsion. Generally, using your blade, wand or finger to create a circle in any object in a spell is recommended. As we work with Hekate as a Three-Formed Goddess, making these circles three times is always beneficial, as is doing anything in a spell three-fold. There are other ways that can manipulate energies during a spell. One of my personal favorites is using knot work.

Hand positions are another part of many rites, such as the kleis used in the Evocation to Hekate. The left hand is typically used to connect with Under World energy and for repulsive magic, while the right does the opposite. The hand position in the evocation can be maintained throughout the incantation of a spell or we can make different gestures to support the spoken incantation.

Timing

When planning your spell, it's vital that you choose the best time to do it whenever possible. I added that caveat because there are times when we must do a spell right away or there are other restrictions on when we can do it. Take the phases of the lunar cycle, astrological energies and the days of the week into consideration when developing a spell. Generally, starting your spell planning at Noumenia with the goal of doing the spell on the Full Moon is recommended, unless your working needs to capitalize on the energies of the waxing or waning phases. Another way that time is involved in spells is the use of the past, present and future. For example, we can view the past as the energy of the Under World if this time for us was painful. If we are feeling that this pain is holding us back from living an optimal life, then we can ask Hekate to release us from it in a spell. We can use each time period – past, present and future – to correspond to different components of a working. "The past is behind me, the present is mine, and I summon the future of my intention" is a way to look at this idea. Spells can include all three time periods, like in this example, or can focus on one or two of them. If you think about it, spells are always about one of these time periods.

Using Hekate's Symbols in Spells

I've already discussed using keys and the use of Hekate's Wheel for creating sacred space. We can also use the strophalos as a magical focus. For example, if you wanted to get a new job, you could start by pinpointing three specific things that you need to do to get a new position, then you could indicate the three core requirements you need in a new job, and finally you could add the three forces that have to come together in order for this job to manifest. You could use the circles for the latter, the central figure for the requirements, and the coils for your necessary actions. I prefer using the coils for actions because, to me, they are not only symbolic of serpentine energy and rebirth, but of movement – like a tightly wound coil ready to spring into action. You can draw all this onto an actual strophalos, creating a powerful magical object.

Tools of Spell Craft

We often use our magical tools in spells, including the blade, the feather and the wand. Other tools that you use in a spell, such as your fire-wand (i.e., lighter) and a mortar and pestle should be cleansed prior to your working. The blade can be used to symbolically cut ties or for cutting up things. The wand can be used as an energetic focal point, as a bridge between your energy and those evoked during the spell. You can custom build a wand for a specific spell by using correspondences appropriate for your ritual or you can have one that you use for all workings. The feather is both a representative of Air and Sky and can be used to create the "wind" necessary for activating a spell, such as releasing the powers of incense.

Magical Products

The first product that you make when doing a spell is the actual written incantation. In addition, you can make an object or put a group of them together. A singular object of power is referred to as an amulet or magical coin, both can be considered charms. When we group objects together into a magical talisman, there is even more power added to a spell. Amulets and talismans can consist of all sorts of correspondences, and usually should involve one of Hekate's symbols, such as keys or Her Wheel. Her fiery energy is typically involved in a spell as both one of Her symbols and as a potent magical force on its own.

Witch and Spell Bags

Another essential tool for spell crafting is the witch bag. There are two basic categories of witch bags: 1.) For keeping magical supplies, 2.) For carrying offerings and other ritual things, and 3.) For storing things associated with a specific working. Most of the time, we can keep our tools right on the altar. Plus, we often have objects being consecrated in the Salt Strophalos. Once these items are prepared for use, it's a good idea to have a designated place to keep them. If you don't have a lot of things, then a witch bag is suitable, but if you have plenty then you'll need a special box or cupboard. If you're going to be carrying your purified items or your tools with you, a bag will come in handy. This bag can be used for carrying your offerings to the crossroads, too.

Witch Bags

There are so many ways to make your own witch bag for storing supplies and for transporting ritual items. I recommend that you have two separate bags, although you can start with one. I have a bag for keeping objects and tools in that are not currently being used, then I have one that is an on-standby bag ready to add ritual items to for doing my monthly Deipnon crossroads working. You can start with a plain black bag and use paint markers to customize it using Hekate's symbols, epithets and correspondences. I have special protective charms that I keep on all my witch bags. Keys are a great item to use as a charm. You can charge the key in your Salt Strophalos and infuse it with protective energy by smoking it using the Three Keys Incense. Say a protective incantation over it. Be creative with your bag choice. The one I use for portable workings is a black nylon satchel covered in red roses. You should have small jars for storing herbs and offerings that can easily fit into your bigger bag. You might even want to have a second set of the three tools we work with in Modern Hekatean Witchcraft in there, too. Inside your big witch bag, you'll often have the smaller ones we use for specific spells.

Spell Bags

Spell bags are used to contain the correspondences used in a working. We can use one to store items as we prepare them for our spell to get them free of nonessential energy. During a spell, we can put the correspondences in one as we recite the incantation. For attraction magic, the spell bag is carried with us while the working manifests. When doing a removal spell, the bag is destroyed or disposed of once it contains the energy of the working. Spell bags can be just about any sort of small bag. I have a bunch on hand. I also keep fabric that I cut into squares and then tie around the spell ingredients. For any specific spell, you can select an epithet, a botanical and a stone or crystal and then put them into a spell bag while reciting an incantation.

The Well-Stocked Witch's Cupboard

I am a relentless collector of all sorts of things that I use in witchcraft, from animal carcasses to seaweed and everything in between. The basics include the Three Key Herbs, salt, charcoal (activated and burning), egg shells (great for any manifesting work), bones (for working with Under World currents), etc. I have a collection of keys at the ready as well. I use one on my incenses and potions after infusing with my intention and asking Hekate's blessing over it. I maintain an assortment of the different colors, a collection of herbs, way too many stones and crystals, and lots of other correspondences. Having a separate set of pots, utensils and bowls is vital for crafting witch waters and potions. Have on mortar and pestle for blending consumable botanicals and a separate one for toxins. You don't want to accidentally poison anyone. I've already mentioned keeping bags, fabric and jars on hand. Clays, paints, markers and inks in various colors are great to have on hand. Beeswax candles and candles in various colors, especially black are a necessity. I burn a black candle and a big beeswax one everyday to keep the household energies in balance. You should also have a supply of the magic water made from the three key herbs on hand. You can use this as the basis for potions. Add herbs, stones and other ingredients to the water that have the energetic properties associated with your working.

The Elements and Spells

In modern witchcraft, the four elements of air, earth, fire and water are involved in many workings. We can call upon the four elements when we begin a spell or to help create sacred space and we can use their energies in our workings. Hekate is directly associated with three of them through Her dominion over land, sea and sky. The fourth, fire, is one of Her most potent symbols.

Air

By now, the idea of the power of breath is well known to you because of your regular practice of the Hekate's Breath Chant. We use our breath to help us remain balanced, centered and grounded. Breath in magic is so important. Along with blood, it is the vital essence of our bodies. You can write breathwork into an incantation. For example, you can use a cycle of three breaths to add power. We often blow on the written incantation to activate it and the act of blowing out a candle is used in the same way. Wind magic involves calling upon this force to carry your spell out into the world where it shall be manifested. This is especially helpful if you are doing a working that requires involving forces outside of your home. You can call upon the wind directly and envision the spell being directed by it to the desired location. Air represents the Sky and is thus associated with Hekate as Gatekeeper and the Upper World.

Earth

We can take crossroads dirt and mix it into our spells, either by sprinkling it over our written incantations or mixing it into our herbals. Burying incantations and magical objects are often done at the end of a spell with an intention to either grow something (using seed energy) or to lay something to rest. Earth represents Hekate as Guide and the Middle World.

Fire Magic

Fire, of course, is one of the major parts of any working. We almost always light candles during a ritual of any type. We burn incense, releasing the energetic properties of the herbs involved. Often, we burn the incantation or another object as an additional type of releasing magic. Fire scrying is something you're already familiar with. In terms of the association with Hekate, fire symbolizes the World Soul and the Liminal Realm.

Candle Magic

If you are unable to light candles, then battery operated ones will be fine. You can account for this lackluster energy source by ensuring that the correspondences you use are exceptionally appropriate to your working. In Modern Hekatean Witchcraft, candle magic works in the two ways I've already mentioned, but we can further elevate the contribution of them by choosing the most appropriate colors for our spells. If candles in the actual colors aren't available, you can paint the color onto the candle or use a neutral color with a candle holder of the appropriate hue.

I recommend using beeswax candles, both because they were used historically in workings with Hekate and because they are less toxic than other kinds.

Water

Water is symbolic of Hekate as Guardian and the Under World. The depths of the oceans are as unknown to humanity as this realm. Mysterious, dark but necessary for human life. We use water in our potions, including magical waters. We purify ourselves with water and we can use this symbolism in our magic. Thus, water can be included in a spell where the intention requires something to be "washed clean." In the same way that we clean ourselves up, we can immerse our fears, harmful thoughts or bad habits into a black bowl containing water. This also works well to get rid of toxic people or things if you rip up an image of them into the bowl while concentrating on having the energy of the water remove them from your life. Dispose of this muddy water quickly after your working, getting it off your property. There's a convenient device in your bathroom for doing this! I want to mention that using blue to represent water energy is entirely appropriate and you could also use it for the sky. Ensure that you fuse the appropriate energy into using blue in these ways. This also applies to all the other colors.

You can use samples of the actual elements or work with their symbols by including them in your sigils, drawn on potions or witch bags, etc. Those are a few ways that the elements can be involved.

Casting a Spell

You've learned about all the parts of a spell, except for activation and dismissal or devocation. The former refers to any energetic activities you do immediately prior to casting Hekate's Wheel or another type of circle. This includes lighting candles or incense that are not directly involved during your invocation. At the end of the incantation comes the devocation, the words you say to express gratitude and to bid farewell to Hekate.

After the Spell

Spell clean-up includes disposing of any objects that need to be done away with, like burying things and the practical tasks of putting reusable objects back in the Salt Strophalos for cleansing and tidying up the space. As soon as possible after the spell is finished, record your experiences – what went well, what didn't, your feelings and thoughts, and any messages you may have received. Be sure to do a self check-up regarding your cognitive, emotional and physical states. If you are feeling too wonky, use your grounding and centering techniques to get back in shape. The spell follow-up consists of the things that you committed to doing during the incantation. It's a good idea to make a plan with a timeline to ensure that you're doing everything necessary in the mundane world to manifest your goal. Magic doesn't work unless we make it! Carrying your amulet or talisman with you is a great reminder. Track your progress and make a record of magical interventions. Spell evaluation is an important part of witchcraft.

Exercise: Writing and Casting Your Own Spell

This course has given you all that you need to craft your own highly effective spells. Record everything from start to finish. If you are new to spell crafting, I suggest that you start with something straightforward, like in the examples given. Sometimes, we can take on too elaborate a project, including spells, and there's no point in doing that. Don't be afraid to scrap one that seems wonky or to make up your own correspondences. Do your research, think things through and be confident. There's not much for me to say, except that I love creating and casting spells, and I hope you do, too.

Summary

Witchcraft is about seeking to control the outcome of a situation. We use our power to cast spells that help us attain our goals, whether it's for attracting a new partner or sending healing energy. Spell crafting includes all the different components of a magical working including: spell category, intention, incantation, words of power, correspondences, activities and timing. The basic types of spells are: attraction, banishing, binding, healing, manifestation, mediumship, protection, reversal and transmutation. The intention is the most important part of any spell but believing in your own power is even more vital. Magical tools are often included in a spell, in Modern Hekatean Witchcraft the core ones are the blade, the feather and the wand. The elements are an additional source of energy that can be included in our workings. Colors and candle magic further increase the power of a spell. There are several parts to a spell that need to be adhered to ensure our intended outcome is manifested. Putting all this together, you can craft your own powerful spell.

Becoming a Keeper of Her Keys:
Self-Initiation

To me, having an intimate initiation ritual where it's just you and Hekate is so reflective of what Modern Hekatean Witchcraft is all about. While teachers (of which I am one) are vital to our development, it is ultimately ourselves who run our own personal temple. With this initiation, you become the priestess or priest of your sanctuary.

Planning Initiation

Before we get into our discussion about solitary practice, I want to give you the heads-up about your upcoming initiation. If you're following the recommended schedule, then you will have recently completed your monthly Deipnon ritual. Hopefully, you're reading this on Noumenia which means everything is perfectly in line for doing your ritual on the next one. This Noumenia you should set the intention to have a beautiful and transformative initiation and seek Hekate's blessing upon it. This is followed on the Full Moon by the first phase of becoming a Keeper of Her Keys, The Key of Initiation Journey. After this is the time to complete the Initiation Self-Test and to develop your Initiation Ritual which will be conducted on the next Noumenia. On the day before, you'll complete the Deipnon of the Initiate. If everything works out according to schedule, you'll be doing the Initiation Ceremony a year and a day after beginning the course, in keeping with the tradition for the cycle of witchcraft training.

Initiation is a form of rebirth. The journey to receive your key of initiation should take place on the Full Moon. This will give you a couple of weeks to develop your initial ritual. On the Deipnon in between the journey and the initiation, you should focus your devotional activities on expressing your gratitude to Hekate in terms of what this course has brought out in you. I believe that this course does just that – it brings out what you already know in your soul. Hekate brought you to this place and you were willing to take that key from Her. Now it is time to become a priest or priestess of your own temple.

Solitary Practice

Overseeing your own temple is a wonderful thing. You have complete control over what activities take place. If you want to change things up, there's no committee to deal with. I believe that solitary practice requires some sort of community though. You may already be involved in the Keeping Her Keys online world, but if you aren't, I recommend that you connect with us. Having a group of people to share your practice of Modern Hekatean Witchcraft with will benefit your individual work immensely. If you're involved with groups that don't enhance your practice (and your life in general), then you might want to consider leaving them. As a solitary witch, you need to ensure that those that you associate with support you in the same way that a witch in a coven needs to be supported.

Modern life

Our ability to interact with other devotees around the globe is a huge plus of contemporary life. In addition, there is a growing acceptance of witchcraft in most of western society. This doesn't mean that it is 100% safe to proclaim yourself a witch. Becoming your own priest or priestess means governing your expression of your status as you so choose. There's no obligation to come out of the broom closet if you're not ready. Even within the pagan universe, there are some who view us Hekateans with anxiety. In my experience, this is usually because we are clever, critical thinkers who worship a goddess that is both fierce and free. If you run into people who criticize your practice of Modern Hekatean Witchcraft, remember our principles. Even when cursing an enemy, we do this out of kindness – even if it's compassion towards those hurt by the recipient of our hexing. There are also those who resist this understanding. That's their problem, not yours. You have better things to do.

Personal development

The most important rule of witchcraft is to know yourself. Therefore, personal development work is so important in Modern Hekatean Witchcraft. The better we know our own mind, the more effective we can be in our witchery. In this course, you've learned many different strategies designed to help you gain insight and to increase your self-discipline. You've got all the skills you need to handle difficult encounters, from your meditation practice to your spell casting abilities and your close connection with Hekate. Also apply these skills to all areas of your life, including your relationships and plans. Continue with your Witch's Hour of Power and change it up to reflect your current interests. Daily journaling with an eye to how you are doing with the principles is important. The more we work on ourselves, the more effective our witchcraft becomes and the deeper our bond with Hekate.

Honoring Hekate

By now you've realized that our devotional activities to Hekate are of immense benefit to ourselves as well. When we hold Hekate in esteem, we are also honoring our own inner goddess or god. Continuing to follow the monthly Deipnon and Noumenia rituals will further your practice. In addition, you should follow the monthly and seasonal sabbats. You can adhere to the recommendations of this course or adapt things as you feel led. Always do what makes the most sense to you.

The Importance of Sovereignty

Over two decades ago when I first got serious about witchcraft I was taught that a witch serves no man. This teaching was born from the centuries of persecution that witches faced. The freedom we have today was washed in their blood. We have a solemn duty to remember our ancestors. One way that we do this is by maintaining our sovereignty in all areas of our lives. Living the principles helps us to honor the dead, too. As does being a devotee of the Queen of the Witches. Hekate will not force you to do anything truly against your will, even if it would be in your best interests. She respects our sovereignty, and we respect our own and that of others.

Mentors and Teachers

Being a sovereign witch involves continuous learning, as we are curious creatures. When selecting a mentor or a teacher, do your research and use your intuition before committing to anything. There will be times when you are hungry to learn more and are desperately seeking out a teacher to help you. That mentor will appear when the time is right. Trust in the process. Don't rush into courses in haste. Remember that you are your own greatest teacher.

The Meaning of Initiation

Initiation is the process through which you acknowledge your proficiency as a witch. It is evidence of a certain level of skill as a practitioner of Modern Hekatean Witchcraft. While you've acquired the knowledge necessary to become an initiate through the content of the course, you've also gained deep understanding of Hekate, witchcraft and yourself. The two combine to produce wisdom, the true gift of initiation. Initiation also infers a serious personal commitment to practicing Modern Hekatean Witchcraft.

Requirements for Initiation

Given that this is a self-initiation, you alone determine the requirements. The self-test at the end of this chapter should be completed prior to beginning the initiation process.

Preparing for Initiation

The self-test is part of your initiation preparations. It is not meant to be a "pass or fail" exam but rather an opportunity for self-evaluation of the concepts taught in this course. Use your journal, Book of Shadows and the lessons to help you complete it. If there are areas where you feel that you're lacking, take time to review them. There are other things to be done before initiation. Like with any ritual, you need to prepare the offerings, altar, your personal hymn or prayer and your robe. While a robe is not required for initiation, it is highly recommended that you are dressed in comfortable red clothes. I'm mentioning this now in case you need to sort out your wardrobe. You're familiar with the process for preparing objects, tools and how to write your hymn or prayer. Scheduling the initiation includes the time for taking the self-test, time to write the hymn or prayer, the journey to receive your Key of Initiation from Hekate and the final ritual. You'll need an actual key for this ritual. You should have fresh salt for the strophalos and enough to stand on. You'll also need a red cloth to stand on. The candles should be black, red and white. You can use the Three Keys Incense or your own blend. If your robe doesn't have a hood, you should find a scarf or veil to wear. Speaking of things, you'll be wearing, you'll also need a cord or chain for the key. Finally, many practitioners purchase or make a new image of Hekate for their altar as part of the initiation process.

The Key of Initiation Journey

Initiation consists of two parts – the initiation by Hekate and your self-initiation ceremony. The Key of Initiation Journey is where you'll receive the gift of initiation from Hekate. The two weeks between the Key of Initiation journey to Noumenia may be a time of intense downloads of information from Our Lady. When we are receiving this sort of spiritual upgrade, it's vital to maintain our daily meditation practice. Do the balancing, centering and grounding practices as much as you need to. Also, keep a record of everything that you feel and observe. Your regular journaling process is crucial during these two weeks. For the Key of Initiation journey, you don't need anything special.

The Key of Initiation Journey

You should do a ritual purification of yourself and the space in which you will be doing this journey. The space should be comfortable – either lying down on a blanket on the floor or sitting in a relaxed position. I recommend a ritual bath with Epsom salts and herbs such as frankincense, lavender and olive oil. To cleanse the space, you should tidy it up as much as possible and burn the initiation incense consisting of our Three Keys Incense plus one that represents Hekate as the World Soul and one that is personally meaningful to you. I prefer the resins such as benzoin, frankincense and myrrh to represent myself if I am already using mugwort in the mix. For Hekate as the World Soul, I typically use rose petals. Set aside at least one hour for the journey and processing it afterwards.

Once you and your space are purified, you are ready to begin. If you are following the text, perhaps making your own recording of it, then I suggest using music that is appropriate.

In this journey you will travel to the Liminal Realm, the mysterious hidden world that Hekate calls home. In the journey, She will welcome you as an initiate of Her mysteries, as a practitioner of Modern Hekatean Witchcraft and will bestow upon you the title of Keeper of Her Keys. She will give you a key. This key is unlike any other that you have previously received for it unlocks wisdom deep within you. As I'm sitting here writing this, I'm tearing up because when Our Lady brought this journey to me I was so overcome with Her and the key She gave me that has enabled me to share this course with you. This is a beautiful, transformative journey. Many blessings to you as you venture forth.

Your Vision of Hekate

The journey text is intentionally vague when describing Hekate, so you can receive your own vision of her. While preparing for the journey, try not to think of images that you've seen, instead keep a blank space regarding her appearance. Hekate has many different roles and characteristics. Her physical appearance reflects these various aspects. When you meet Hekate on this journey, take time to observe her physical appearance very closely. After the journey write a description of her appearance using as much detail as possible. There will be important clues about both your understanding of Hekate and your relationship with her that will be shown through the way she chooses to present herself to you.

The Gift of Initiation

After you meet Hekate, She will give you a key. This key of initiation represents the next phase of your development as a practitioner of Modern Hekatean Witchcraft. The key is a symbol of your rebirth as a priestess or priest of your own sanctuary, as a Guide who can mentor others, and as a Keeper of Her Keys. As you receive the key, take notice of your thoughts and feelings, as well as any words that Hekate speaks to you. After the journey, describe your immediate interpretations of the key and any messages that you received. Coupled with your vision, the key will provide great insight.

Other Parts of the Journey

The journey begins with you entering the Liminal Realm that exists between the three worlds. You'll remain in the Liminal Realm, leaving behind the everyday life of the Middle World and not entering either the Under World or the Upper World. The center of Hekate is found in this space. Hekate is represented by the color gold while you are silver. Black signifies the energy of the Under World and emotions. The Upper World is the realm of thoughts and is represented by white. Red, the color of the life force, indicates the Middle World. As you are in the Liminal Realm between all three worlds, the energy is comprised of these sources.

Experiences during the Journey

While you are on your journey, you may feel intense emotions and have profound thoughts. This is because you are entering the core of Hekate's energy. Take note of these experiences while on the journey. Once you notice them, tell them you'll return to them later after you've completed the working. You want to stay focused on experiencing a vision of Hekate and receiving your key. You are completely safe in the Liminal Realm. Hekate wouldn't grant you admission unless you are ready.

Let Your Journey Begin

Begin the journey by getting comfortable. Then close your eyes. Prepare to leave the everyday world by counting yourself down into a state of deep relaxation, starting at your feet with the number 13 and working your way up to the number 1 at your crown. While counting, breathe in slow deep breaths that both cleanse and relax your entire being. Become aware of the energy within your feet and beneath your feet, then let it go. Repeat this process as you move up through your body while counting down. Feel the energy through all the parts of your body and your surroundings. Noticing it, then releasing it. At your crown, you release your thoughts.

After you've released your thoughts, you enter a state of disconnection from your physical body and your surroundings. The everyday world falls away from you. You are alert, but relaxed. Open to the experience you are about to have.

Entering the Liminal Realm

As you slip into the Liminal Realm, you once again become

aware of your body. There is a sense of weightlessness, but you are deeply connected to the place where you now are. Open your eyes in this new world. Take your time here as you enter your liminal body. You become aware of your breathing, your heart rate. Your arms, legs and torso. Here you are fully in your liminal form. You are lightness filled with a sense of great power. Your feet are connected to the earth beneath them, lightly and softly. Your head reaches up towards the heavens.

Begin by noticing the shimmering silver sandals upon your feet. Next, turn your attention to your left wrist that's surrounded by a band of black pearls. On your right wrist is a similar band of white pearls. Reaching up with both hands, you feel a band of red pearls around your neck. The energy of the realms radiates through the pearls, connecting with your own life force, creating a sense of balance and wholeness. Power. Contentment. Awareness. As you let go of the red pearls, you notice your robe. It's a shimmering crimson, the color of the life force. The hood covers your head.

Extend your perception out from your being to your immediate surroundings. You are at the threshold of the three worlds. Immediately behind you is the door to the Middle World of everyday life. Take a step away from this door as it silently closes behind you. To your left, you see the Gates of the Under World, guarded by two black dogs. These gates are closed to you. On your right, the Gates of the Upper World stand closed with the serpent of creation before them. Neither the dogs nor the serpent causes you alarm. You understand that they are Hekate's representatives. They remain subdued in your presence, for they already know why you are here.

You are at peace knowing that the three realms are closed off to you. Safe in the knowledge that you can return to the Middle World at any time. That you are well-prepared for this moment and very welcome. You are aware that you can travel to the Under World and the Upper World when it is necessary.

See these two Realms as the future, where you'll go to further understand Hekate's Mysteries.

You are at the Crossroads of the Three Worlds, standing on the threshold of the Liminal Realm, the sacred space of the Goddess Hekate. The space is dark with no moon, stars or sun to be seen. The energy is charged with that of the three realms.

Now you look ahead to the path of alabaster, jasper and obsidian stones immediately in front of you. The smells of the Liminal Realm comfort you with their mixture of roses, herbs and a hint of the warm scent of decay.

Torches light your way ahead. As you begin to walk down the path, take in your surroundings. What plants do you see? What thoughts come to mind? What feelings are you having? Take notice of these things, then release them. You'll return to them after your journey.

As you walk the path, you become aware of the black, red and white energy currents flowing from you and all around you. Although the energy is strong, you remain calm as you are one with the currents.

You reach the end of the path. Looking up, you realize that there is a figure standing before you, on the steps of a temple. On her feet are the most beautiful golden sandals. She beckons you towards her. As you approach, you take in her appearance, savoring the details to remember later. This is the Hekate of your understanding. This is how she has chosen to present herself to you.

You stand before her now. Say your given name. She says your new name back to you; this is the one She has chosen for you. You stand in her presence, absorbing her divine energy. Take your time in this moment. Take notice of any messages that she gives you, storing them to memory for later processing.

You feel powerful, weightless, whole and content in her presence.

She raises her hand, revealing the most precious key.

This is the key that she is giving to you now, granting you a personal understanding of who she is.

She steps toward you. Her intense energy surrounds you like a blanket, mingling her golden nature with the black, red and white of the realms and your silver.

She removes your hood, gently kissing your forehead as she does. Holding your hand, she gently places the key in it, closing your fist over it.

The kiss and the key spread throughout your body, infusing you with her golden energy and the knowledge bestowed in the key. This is Hekate's gift to you. Your own understanding of her. Unique. Special. Purified. Whole.

She raises your hood, then steps back from you. You can now see the glorious ring of keys that she wears. These are your future keys that will come to you in due course.

Pause here. Feeling the energy of the kiss and key pulsing through your every cell. Study the key in your hand. As you finish committing the details to memory, the key is slowly absorbed into your hand. With the key now part of you, you look up to discover that Hekate is no longer visible to you. This doesn't bother you because you now have the key of your own understanding of her within you. She will always be part of you.

When you are ready, take one last look at her temple. Know that you can return when you need to. Slowly turn and walk back down the path. Noticing new details to think about later. Walking past the gates of the Under World and Upper World. Now you stand before the door to the Middle World. You are ready to return to everyday life.

As you open the door to the Middle World, your liminal form slips away replaced by your physical being. Close the door behind you. Return to your body. Feel your breath, your heartbeat. Become aware of the feelings in your body. Your thoughts. You are calm, but alert. Energized yet balanced.

Slowly count your way back to consciousness beginning with

the number 1 at your crown and finishing with the number 12 at your feet. As you count, you become increasingly aware of your body and your surroundings. After you've finishing counting, take your time before moving from the space. Be gentle with yourself.

After the Journey

It's best to record your experiences immediately after you finish the journey. A good idea is to record a voice memo right after and then write about the experience. It will take time to process the experience. Having the recording and your written thoughts will help you immensely.

Self-Evaluation

The self-test of initiation can be found immediately after this chapter. There are questions that evaluate your knowledge of each of the thirteen lessons in this course. Do the evaluation using this text and your notes. However, you should begin the test without consulting either source. Do as much as you can without it. The areas where you need to use the resources to complete should be noted for further study after initiation. This is a test, but not the pass/fail kind. The goal is to complete it in such a way that you can refer to it as a reference for the key concepts of this course.

Declaration of Initiation

Your Declaration of Initiation is the statement that you read during the Initiation Ceremony. There is a basic script provided that you can use, or you can embellish it how you feel led. What's important is that you write a statement that confirms your commitment to the three principles, to Hekate and to the practice of witchcraft. In my experience, this initiation can be very emotional just like the first initiation when you received the key from Hekate. Although you are free to add to the declaration,

I urge you to keep it simple. You should copy it into your Book of Shadows with the other specifics about the Ceremony (date, offerings, etc.) in advance so you can read it from here if you have difficulty remembering it during the ceremony. However, it's best to memorize it – another reason for keeping it simple.

Declaration of Initiation

Mighty Hekate, She who is
Guardian,
Guide
Gatekeeper.
    Mistress, attend me now.
I stand before You, *say your new name,*
I declare that I am committed to living the three principles of
Passion
Kindness
Integrity
I declare that I am committed to honoring you through
Words
    Actions
    Spirit.
I declare that I have met the requirement of initiation through
Study
Exercises
Rituals.
I declare that I have earned this key I place upon my neck. *Place key around neck.*
Mistress, I join this key with that which you have given me.
I declare that my initiation is now complete.
Remove your hood or head covering.
I am reborn as Your Guide,
One of Your Chosen.
Mighty Hekate, She who is
Guardian,

Guide

Gatekeeper.

Blessed Queen, Accept my declaration and gratitude.

The Deipnon of the Initiate

Initiation is a sacred time between you and Hekate. As you experienced during the journey, the feeling of completeness and acceptance can be very emotional. You may still feel this way as your get ready to the do the last part of initiation. However, you'll recall that initiation consists of three parts, so don't forget to do the Deipnon of the Initiate Ritual. This is an intensely private rite where you express your gratitude to Hekate for the gift of this course, for your own accomplishment and for Her guidance along your way. I recommend that this is a good time to install a new representation of Hekate on your altar. Refer to the section on preparing Her image. If you don't already have a statue, you may want to make or purchase one for this Deipnon. This Deipnon should be a simple one. Hekate's presence will be strong at the ritual as She will be with you through the entire time from when you receive the Key of Initiation from Her until you complete the Initiation Ceremony tomorrow. I suggest an offering of a simple Hekate's Supper that you deposit at a crossroads. This is the last time you'll do this as an initiate. On the next Deipnon you'll be a Guide, a Keeper of Her Keys and a priestess or priest of your own temple. As always, you should plan this Deipnon carefully and make sure you record your hymn or prayer and the other details in your Book of Shadows.

The Initiation Ceremony

The initiation ceremony is the time to put all your skills as a practitioner of Modern Hekatean Witchcraft to use. Red is worn and stood on to signify your completion of the first course in the Keeping Her Keys framework. You have mastered the skills of the Middle World. This applies to the balanced approach to magic that you've learned during this course, as well as to your achievements in personal development. When you accept your key of self initiation, you become a Guide and a Keeper of Her Keys. You can use "Enodia" as part of the initiation name that Hekate gave to you.

Initiation Ceremony Magical Supply List

- Red clothing, preferably a robe with a hood.
- Red cloth or carpet, big about 3x5.
- Salt – enough to refill your Strophalos and to stand on during the ceremony.
- Three Keys incense.
- Almond or olive oil.
- Your key of initiation on a cord or chain.
- A red candle.
- Altar set up with offering to Hekate.
- Blade, feather, wand.

Initiation Ceremony Procedure

- Begin at sundown on Noumenia.
- Ritual bath, preferably with frankincense for extra purification and to activate your metaphysical abilities.
- Dressing: Red with a head covering (see above). Choose comfortable clothing. If you are okay with it, wear nothing underneath, no lotions, no make-up, etc. Just you and the robe. You can do this sky clad if that's what appeals to you.
- Set-up: In front of your altar, arrange the red carpet or cloth.
- Altar: The salt in your Strophalos needs to be fresh. Once your Ceremony objects and tools are cleansed, use the process previously discussed to clean and refill it. This

is symbolic of your rebirth as a Keeper of Her Keys. On the altar, you should have your blade, feather and wand cleansed and ready. You'll need to have the anointing oil, key and the Declaration of Initiation on hand, as well. For offerings to Hekate, red roses are most appropriate since they signify Hekate as Guide.

- Anointing Oil. During the Initiation Ceremony you will anoint yourself with one of two oils sacred to Hekate, almond or olive. The oil should be of the highest possible quality. Anointing with oil during an initiation ceremony dates to the rites of the ancient priestesses. It is a symbol of Hekate's mark upon you.

Initiation Ceremony

Stand in front of your altar on the red cloth. Cast the strophalos. Do the evocation. Then move onto the Declaration of Initiation:

Mighty Hekate, She who is
Guardian, *(hands down)*
Guide *(hands at heart center)*
Gatekeeper *(hands up)*
    Mistress, attend me now. *(Arms extended in welcome)*
Welcome, Queen of Sea *(hold wand down)*
Welcome, Queen of Sky *(hold feather up)*
Welcome, Queen of Land. *(hold blade at heart center)*
Return tools to the altar. Open arms again,
I stand before You, *say your new name, (light the red candle)*
I declare that I am committed to living the three principles of
    (pick up anointing oil)
Passion *(anoint your feet)*
Kindness *(anoint your heart center)*
Integrity *(anoint your forehead)*
I declare that I am committed to honoring you through
Words *(anoint your feet)*

Actions *(anoint your heart center)*
Spirit. *(Anoint your forehead)*
I declare that I have met the requirement of initiation through
Study *(anoint your feet)*
Exercises *(anoint your heart center)*
Rituals. *(Anoint your forehead)*
I declare that I have earned this key I place upon my neck. *Place*
    key around neck
Mistress, I join this key with that which you have given me.
I declare that my initiation is now complete.
Remove your hood or head covering.
I am reborn as Your Priestess (Priest),
One of Your Chosen.
Mighty Hekate, She who is
Guardian,
Guide.
Gatekeeper.
    Blessed Queen, accept my declaration and gratitude.
    My intention is true
And my will is strong.

Spend as much time as you like standing in this space, as your priesthood descends fully upon you. When you are ready, extinguish the candle and open the space. As always, take time to record your experience in your journal. Be extra kind to yourself for the next few days as you adjust to your priesthood.

Final Words

Congratulations! As a Keeper of Her Keys, you're now part of the growing community of practitioners of Modern Hekatean Witchcraft. Being a Priestess or Priest of the Middle Road means that you are Hekate's representative in Her role as Guide. You are welcome to share the rituals and other workings that you've learned with others. If you choose, you can become involved as a mentor in the Keeping Her Keys community to show the way to others.

Now that you have completed the training of the Middle World, you have developed a special understanding of Hekate as Guide. In the next course, the journey takes you to the Under World where you'll learn about healing, hexing, communication with the dead and other activities of chthonic witchcraft. The final course will find you traveling the starry road to the Upper World with an emphasis on astrological magic, working with angels and ceremonial techniques.

Initiation Self-Test

Lesson 1

1. What are the three keys of Modern Hekatean Witchcraft and what do they mean to you?

2. What does "the holy darkness is nigh" mean? What evidence do you see of this?

3. Now that you've completed this course, what do you perceive to be three benefits of Modern Hekatean Witchcraft?

Lesson 2

4. How has making the commitment to living the Three Principles changed your life.

5. Discuss the role of balancing, centering and grounding before and after magical workings.

Lesson 3

6. Reflect upon the messages that you have received from Hekate throughout this course.

7. How has your ability to connect with Hekate changed throughout this course?

Lesson 4

8. Compare your understanding of Hekate now with what it was when you completed the exercise at the beginning of Lesson 4.

9. Describe the role that your daily meditation practice using the Three Keys Chant has had on your magical and mundane lives.

Lesson 5

10. What is one epithet that you feel called to understand

more?

11. Some people believe that the Book of Shadows should be kept secret, while others freely share theirs. What is your opinion?

Lesson 6

12. Discuss the different levels of Hekate's presence, including spontaneous communication and evocation.

Lesson 7

13. Reflect upon the various seasonal and sabbat rituals you've completed since starting this course.

Lesson 8

14. Which of Hekate's symbols do you feel closest to? Why do you think you feel this way?

Lesson 9

15. Summarize the method of preparing objects and tools for use in workings.
16. How are Hekate's Animals associated with the Realms?

Lesson 10

17. Describe one of the plants in Hekate's garden (in addition to the Three Key Plants) that you have worked with or plan on working with.

Lesson 11

18. How has having a regular Tarot practice impacted your life?

Lesson 12

19. What is the Liminal Realm? Describe your experience of the energy of it.

Lesson 13

20. How are Words of Power used in spells?
21. Compare and contrast the energies of the four elements.

Endnotes

1. Mead, G. R. S., *The Chaldean Oracles*; Theosophical Publishing Society; 1908.
2. Evelyn-White, Hugh G.; (Trans.); *Hesiod: The Homeric Hymns and Homerica*; William Heinemann Ltd; London; 1941.
3. Brannen, Cyndi; Deeper into the Deipnon. Available online: http://www.patheos.com/blogs/keepingherkeys/2018/01/diving-deeper-into-the-deipnon/
4. Evelyn-White, Hugh G.; (Trans.); *Hesiod: The Homeric Hymns and Homerica*; William Heinemann Ltd; London; 1941.
5. Brannen, Cyndi; Honoring Hekate of the Under World. Available online: http://www.patheos.com/blogs/keeping herkeys/2017/11/oh-holy-night-celebrating-hekate-of-the-underworld/
6. Brannen, Cyndi; Hekate's Fires. Available online: http://www.patheos.com/blogs/keepingherkeys/2018/02/hekate-fire-magic-pentacle/
7. The Orphic Hymn to Hekate. Online: http://www.hellenicgods.org/the-orphic-hymn-to-hecate-aekati---hekate
8. Brannen, Cyndi; Making Magic with Hekate's Keys. Available online: http://www.patheos.com/blogs/keeping herkeys/2018/01/the-magic-of-hekates-keys/
9. Betz, Hans Deter (Ed.); *The Greek Magical Papyri in Translation*; 1992; University of Chicago Press; Chicago.
10. d'Este, Sorita, *Circle for Hekate – Volume 1, History and Mythology*; Avalonia; London; 2016.
11. Miller, Frank Justus; *Seneca's Tragedies Volume 1: Hercules Furens, Troades, Medea, Hippolytus, Oedipus*; 1960; Harvard University Press; Cambridge.
12. Edmonds, J.M. (Trans.), *The Greek Bucolic Poets*. LOEB Classical Library, 1912.

13. Mead, G. R. S., *Pistis Sophia*; John M. Watkins; London; 1921.
14. Shakespeare, William; Macbeth. Online: http://shakespeare.mit.edu/macbeth/full.html
15. Crowley, Aleister; Invocation of Hecate. Online: https://www.scribd.com/doc/16067087/Aleister-Crowley-Invocation-of-Hecate
16. Gardner, Gerald B.; *Witchcraft Today*; Rider & Co; London; 1954.
17. Graves, Robert; *The White Goddess: A Historical Grammar of Poetic Myth*; Faber & Faber; London.
18. Halstead, J. The Secret History of the Triple Goddess. Available online: http://www.patheos.com/blogs/allergicpagan/2014/11/15/the-secret-history-of-the-triple-goddess-part-3-will-the-real-triple-goddess-please-stand-up/
19. Johnson, S. I., *Hekate Soteira*; Scholars Pres; Atlanta; 1990.
20. Betz, Hans Deter (Ed.); *The Greek Magical Papyri in Translation*; 1992; University of Chicago Press; Chicago.
21. Mead, G. R. S., *The Chaldean Oracles*; Theosophical Publishing Society; 1908.
22. The Orphic Hymn to Hekate. Online: http://www.hellenicgods.org/the-orphic-hymn-to-hecate-aekati---hekate
23. d'Este, Sorita, *Circle for Hekate – Volume 1, History and Mythology*, Avalonia; London; 2016.
24. Seaton, R. C. (Trans.), *Apollonius Rhodius: Argonautica*; LOEB Classical Library; 1990.
25. Miller, Frank Justus; *Seneca's Tragedies Volume 1: Hercules Furens, Troades, Medea, Hippolytus, Oedipus*; 1960; Harvard University Press; Cambridge.
26. d'Este, Sorita, *Circle for Hekate – Volume 1, History and Mythology*, London; 2016.
27. Gifford, E. H. (Trans.), *Eusebius of Caesarea: Praeparatio Evangelica*; Horatio Hart, London; 1903.
28. Ronan, Stephen (Ed.), *The Goddess Hekate*; Chthonios Books; Hastings; 1992.

29. d'Este, Sorita, *Circle for Hekate – Volume 1, History and Mythology*, Avalonia; London; 2016.

30. Brannen, Cyndi. Hekate: Guardian of the Marginalized. Available online at: http://www.patheos.com/blogs/keeping herkeys/2017/11/hekate-guardian-of-the-marginalized/

31. d'Este, Sorita (Ed.), Various. *Hekate: Her Sacred Fires*. Avalonia, London; 2010.

32. Brannen, Cyndi. Hekate and the Storms of Life. Available online at: http://www.patheos.com/blogs/keepingherkeys/2017/12/hekate-brimo-and-storms/

33. Brannen, Cyndi. Hekate and November: The Holy Darkness is Nigh. Available online at: http://www.patheos.com/blogs/keepingherkeys/2017/11/holy-darkness-nigh-november-month-modern-hekatean-witchcraft/

34. Brannen, Cyndi; Honoring Hekate of the Under World. Available online: http://www.patheos.com/blogs/keeping herkeys/2017/11/oh-holy-night-celebrating-hekate-of-the-underworld/

35. Brannen, Cyndi; Oh, Night Divine: Honoring Hekate of the Crossroads. Available online at: http://www.patheos.com/blogs/keepingherkeys/2017/11/night-divine-honoring-hekate-crossroads-november-30/

36. Goold, G. P. (Trans.), *Propertius' Elegies*. LOEB Classical Library, 1990. Available online.

37. Brannen, Cyndi. A Modern Hekatean Witchcraft Wheel of the Year. Available online at: http://www.patheos.com/blogs/keepingherkeys/2018/01/hekate-wheel-of-the-year/

38. d'Este, Sorita & Rankine, David, *Hekate: Liminal Rites*; Avalonia, London; 2008.

39. Gifford, E. H. (Trans.), *Eusebius of Caesarea: Praeparatio Evangelica*; Horatio Hart, London; 1903.

40. Gifford, E. H. (Trans.), *Eusebius of Caesarea: Praeparatio Evangelica*; Horatio Hart, London; 1903.

41. Colavito, J. (Trans.), *Orphic Argonautica, by pseudo-Orpheus.*

Online: www.argonauts-book.com/oprhic-argonautica.html

42. Kline, A. S. (Trans). *Ovid's Metamorphoses*. Available online: https://www.poetryintranslation.com/klineasovid.php

43. Brannen,Cyndi.Hekate'sGarden:BayLaurel.Availableonline: http://www.patheos.com/blogs/keepingherkeys/2018/02/ hekates-garden-bay-laurel/

44. Evelyn-White, Hugh G.; (Trans.); *Hesiod: The Homeric Hymns and Homerica*; William Heinemann Ltd; London; 1941.

45. d'Este, Sorita & Rankine, David, *Hekate: Liminal Rites*; Avalonia, London; 2008.

46. Colavito, J. (Trans.), *Orphic Argonautica, by pseudo-Orpheus*. Online: www.argonauts-book.com/oprhic-argonautica.html

47. Edmonds, J.M. (Trans.), *The Greek Bucolic Poets*. LOEB Classical Library, 1912.

Additional Prayers

Prayer to Hekate, Mistress of Balance on the Spring Equinox

Hail Hekate Pasikratea, Queen of the Universe.
Hail Hekate Aglaos, Creator of the Sun.
Hail Hekate Erigeneia, Ruler of the Moon.
As Creator of the Sun,
You shine down upon us,
Bringing life to all things,
As Ruler of the Moon,
You light up the darkest nights.
On this day when the day equals the night,
And the sun and moon are balanced,
I honor you as Divine Keeper of Balance.
On this day when the day equals the night,
May I understand the balance of my own life,
That the darkness and the storms
Yield to the winds of change,
Ushering in a new season.
Hekate Enodia, my road
May be a difficult one,
But my faith that all will be born anew is strong.
I offer my gratitude, Blessed Hekate.
Hail Hekate Pasikratea, Queen of the Universe.
Hail Hekate Aglaos, Creator of the Sun.
Hail Hekate Erigeneia, Ruler of the Moon.

Hymn to Hekate the Powerful on the Summer Solstice

Bright Hekate, Kratais!
All Powerful Goddess, Queen of the Sun!
Hail to You, Fairest Bestower!
Your bounty spreads over the land.
Great Pammetor, Mother of All,
I see you in all the splendor.
Mighty Aglaos, Creatrix of the Sun,
Continue to shine upon my life
And all the world.
I stand here in Your Powerful Light,
And claim my own!
Hail Bright Hekate, Kratais!

Prayer to Hekate of the Harvest on the Fall Equinox

Hail Hekate, Mighty Ruler of Land, Sea and Sky,
From whom all blessings flow!
Hail Hekate, Mighty Ruler of Land, Sea and Sky,
From whom all blessings flow!
Hail Hekate, Mighty Rule of Land, Sea and Sky,
From whom all blessings flow!
For the bounty of the harvest,
Of Land, Sea and Sky,
Hear my gratitude.
For the bounty of the harvest,
Of the material world,
I thank you.
For the bounty of the harvest,
Of my life,
I thank you.
Hail Hekate, Mighty Ruler of Land, Sea and Sky,
From whom all blessings flow!
Hail Hekate, Mighty Ruler of Land, Sea and Sky,
From whom all blessings flow!
Hail Hekate, Mighty Rule of Land, Sea and Sky,
From whom all blessings flow!

Winter Solstice Hymn to Hekate

Hail Hekate Chthonia,
Queen of the Underworld,
Who heard Persephone when no one else did.
Hail Hekate Propolos,
Queen of the Middle World,
Who guided her back to the middle world
Creating the seasons.
Hail Hekate Soteira,
Queen of the Upper World,
Return to me as the wheel of the year turns.
I honor you on the winter solstice,
As you guided Persephone,
Deliver me from darkness.

Hekate Kourotrophos: Blessing of Children

Hail Hekate Soteira,
She who reigns over all creation.
Hail Hekate Pammetor,
The Great Mother of all creatures.
I call upon you as Hekate Kourotrophos,
Guardian of Children.

I ask for Your protection over _____ (list the
names of the children; do each child one at a time).
May Your light shine before them and around them.
Bestow upon my Your principles so that I may protect
_____ *(child's name).
May I honor You through my relationship with this child.

Hail Hekate Kourotrophos,
Guardian of the Children.
May my gratitude for Your protection over these young lives
Be expressed through every part of my life.
Hail Hekate Pammetor,
Great Mother.
Thanks be to You.
Hail Hekate Soteira,
Our Savior.

*As you ask for protection for each child, make an offering in
that child's name. I recommend a clove of garlic. Also, you can
have a talisman for each child in which you focus your energy
and Hekate's, comingling and charging that token. The talisman
can be given to the child to wear or carry with them. I also have
a talisman on my altar to Hekate for each child that I place under
Her care. If you do not have children in your life, you can refer
to all children.

Prayer to Hekate the Storm Bringer

Hail Hekate Brimo,
Hail Hekate the Fierce,
Hail Hekate the Terrifying.
May I be prepared for the storms of life,
May I honor You through my actions,
May I learn from your gifts.
Guide me through life's storms,
Remind me that I am strong beyond measure,
As I weather the chaos.
Grateful I am
For the terrors You send my way,
As I grow wise and fierce.
Hail Hekate Brimo, Storm Bringer
Hail Hekate the Fierce,
Hail Hekate the Terrifying.

Prayer to Hekate, Goddess of the Under World

Hail Hekate Chthonia, Queen of the Under World!
Hail Mighty Lampadios, My Guardian and Goddess!
Light my way.
Hear my humble gratitude for your protection
During my darkest times.
Accept my heartfelt praise for your gifts of
Under World energy,
May I know that the darkness is not to be feared,
But is the realm of birth,
And the depths of my heart.
Hail Hekate Chthonia, Queen of the Under World!
Hail Mighty Lampadios, My Guardian and Goddess!

About the Author

Cyndi Brannen, PhD teaches and writes about Applied Modern Witchcraft. She's a witch and spiritual teacher dedicated to Hekate, her two sons and living the coastal life in rural Nova Scotia. A trained energetic healer, psychic and herbalist, Cyndi also is an internationally-recognized expert on women's health and the development of self-help programs. In 2005, she founded Open Circle Wellness which offers courses and individual support, including the popular Shadow Taming Workshop and Tarot Readings. She developed The Real Work and its newest incarnation, The Sacred Seven: A Magickal Path of Applied Modern Witchcraft. Cyndi has taught meditation and mindfulness to a variety of groups and organizations. She started Keeping Her Keys to fulfill her mission and dream of writing and teaching about Applied Modern Witchcraft and Hekate. She writes the Keeping Her Keys blog at Patheos.com. To learn more about Cyndi and Modern Hekatean Witchcraft, visit Keepingherkeys.com

Acknowledgements

A course like this is the result of many people. I want to start by thanking all the members of the Keeping Her Keys community and those who have participated in Open Circle events and workshops. Everything in this course is based on things I've done with those groups. I am so humbled by each one of you. Your courage, strength and commitment to live a magical life inspire me daily. For my fellow Hekateans, I thank you for the support and for sharing your knowledge. I am forever indebted to Sara Croft who created the amazing database of Hekate's epithets. Sara, I sit here looking at the spreadsheet I made based largely on your research and I bow down to you! To Sorita d'Este has done so much to bring Hekate to the world, I thank you. I am honored to contribute to The Goddess Hekate Facebook page that you created. The third "goddess" that contributed to the creation of this course is my dear Mustard (Lisa). Over the years, she has gone along with my outlaw version of witchcraft, listened to my rants, and has often been my muse. To my beloved mentor and confidante, Willow, I will be forever grateful that you walked up a big hill on a chilly day. To my fabulous sister who has supported me. My dear mother has taught me so much and helped me in immeasurable ways. I also want to pay tribute to my departed Aunt Val, who was very much opposed to anything to do with the occult and witchcraft, nevertheless, taught me to be a stubborn, hard working and opinionated woman through her example. In this way, she is directly responsible for *Keeping Her Keys: Hekate's Modern Witchcraft*. Now that she's on the other side, she understands my strange ways much better.

To my sons, I am forever grateful for your patience, support and being the lights of my life. This book is for both of you.

Lastly, and most importantly, I pay tribute to Hekate.

My life has been transformed since She called me. Keeping Her Keys is my expression of gratitude. Hail Hekate!

Keep on Keeping Her Keys,
Cyndi Brannen

**MOON
BOOKS**

PAGANISM & SHAMANISM

What is Paganism? A religion, a spirituality, an alternative
belief system, nature worship? You can find support for all these
definitions (and many more) in dictionaries, encyclopaedias, and
text books of religion, but subscribe to any one and the truth will
evade you. Above all Paganism is a creative pursuit, an encounter
with reality, an exploration of meaning and an expression of the
soul. Druids, Heathens, Wiccans and others, all contribute their
insights and literary riches to the Pagan tradition. Moon Books
invites you to begin or to deepen your own encounter, right here,
right now.

If you have enjoyed this book, why not tell other readers by
posting a review on your preferred book site.

Recent bestsellers from Moon Books are:

Journey to the Dark Goddess
How to Return to Your Soul
Jane Meredith
Discover the powerful secrets of the Dark Goddess and
transform your depression, grief and pain into healing
and integration.
Paperback: 978-1-84694-677-6 ebook: 978-1-78099-223-5

Shamanic Reiki
Expanded Ways of Working with Universal Life Force Energy
Llyn Roberts, Robert Levy
Shamanism and Reiki are each powerful ways of healing; together,
their power multiplies. Shamanic Reiki introduces techniques to
help healers and Reiki practitioners tap ancient healing wisdom.
Paperback: 978-1-84694-037-8 ebook: 978-1-84694-650-9

Pagan Portals – The Awen Alone
Walking the Path of the Solitary Druid
Joanna van der Hoeven
An introductory guide for the solitary Druid, The Awen Alone
will accompany you as you explore, and seek out your own place
within the natural world.
Paperback: 978-1-78279-547-6 ebook: 978-1-78279-546-9

A Kitchen Witch's World of Magical Herbs & Plants
Rachel Patterson
A journey into the magical world of herbs and plants, filled with
magical uses, folklore, history and practical magic. By popular
writer, blogger and kitchen witch, Tansy Firedragon.
Paperback: 978-1-78279-621-3 ebook: 978-1-78279-620-6

Medicine for the Soul
The Complete Book of Shamanic Healing
Ross Heaven
All you will ever need to know about shamanic healing and how to become your own shaman...
Paperback: 978-1-78099-419-2 ebook: 978-1-78099-420-8

Shaman Pathways – The Druid Shaman
Exploring the Celtic Otherworld
Danu Forest
A practical guide to Celtic shamanism with exercises and techniques as well as traditional lore for exploring the Celtic Otherworld.
Paperback: 978-1-78099-615-8 ebook: 978-1-78099-616-5

Traditional Witchcraft for the Woods and Forests
A Witch's Guide to the Woodland with Guided Meditations and Pathworking
Melusine Draco
A Witch's guide to walking alone in the woods, with guided meditations and pathworking.
Paperback: 978-1-84694-803-9 ebook: 978-1-84694-804-6

Wild Earth, Wild Soul
A Manual for an Ecstatic Culture
Bill Pfeiffer
Imagine a nature-based culture so alive and so connected, spreading like wildfire. This book is the first flame...
Paperback: 978-1-78099-187-0 ebook: 978-1-78099-188-7

Naming the Goddess

Trevor Greenfield

Naming the Goddess is written by over eighty adherents and scholars of Goddess and Goddess Spirituality.

Paperback: 978-1-78279-476-9 ebook: 978-1-78279-475-2

Shapeshifting into Higher Consciousness

Heal and Transform Yourself and Our World with Ancient Shamanic and Modern Methods

Llyn Roberts

Ancient and modern methods that you can use every day to transform yourself and make a positive difference in the world.

Paperback: 978-1-84694-843-5 ebook: 978-1-84694-844-2

Readers of ebooks can buy or view any of these bestsellers by clicking on the live link in the title. Most titles are published in paperback and as an ebook. Paperbacks are available in traditional bookshops. Both print and ebook formats are available online.

Find more titles and sign up to our readers' newsletter at http://www.johnhuntpublishing.com/paganism
Follow us on Facebook at https://www.facebook.com/MoonBooks and Twitter at https://twitter.com/MoonBooksJHP